Magic Moments™

Super Science With Your Kids

Written by Patricia A. Staino
Illustrated by Marilynn G. Barr
Science material edited by Suzanne Moore

The Education Center, Inc.
Greensboro, North Carolina

For Karen
for her "love" of science!

©1997 by THE EDUCATION CENTER, INC.
All rights reserved except as noted below.

Library of Congress Cataloging-in-Publication Data

Staino, Patricia A., 1970–
    Super science with your kids / written by Patricia A. Staino ;
illustrated by Marilynn G. Barr.
        p.   cm. — (Magic moments)
    Includes index.
    Summary: Includes over one hundred science experiments designed to
reinforce math skills and to encourage working with others as well
as to foster understanding of scientific concepts.
    ISBN 1-56234-176-6 (pbk.)
    1. Science—Experiments—Juvenile literature. 2. Scientific
recreations—Juvenile literature. [1. Science—Experiments.
2. Scientific recreations. 3. Experiments.] I. Barr, Marilynn G.,
ill. II. Title. III. Series: Magic moments (Greensboro, N.C.)
Q164.S64   1997
507.8—dc21   97-28320
                                                      CIP
                                                      AC

Cover design by Clevell Harris

The Education Center, Inc.
P.O. Box 9753
Greensboro, NC 27429-0753

Manufactured in the United States

10 9 8 7 6 5 4 3 2 1

SUPER SCIENCE!
WITH YOUR KIDS

Table of Contents

Table of Contents

Dear Kids,

Science is all around you. When you turn on the light, when the leaves fall off the trees, when you pedal your bicycle forward, that's science. You can figure out all sorts of things about the world if you understand a few scientific ideas.

In this book you'll make toys, learn magic tricks, and bake some goodies. And when you're all finished, you'll know a bunch of new stuff about electricity, energy, your body, plants, the sun, and a whole lot more.

Here are a few tips to get you started. They are the **4 Bs** of science:

- **Be safe.** Any time you try something new, you should take it slow and pay attention. Make sure a grown-up is around when you do your experiments, in case you need some help.

- **Be neat.** Some experiments can get messy. It's a good idea to put newspapers down on tabletops and on the floor in case you spill something, and wear old clothes. And be sure to clean up as soon as you are finished.

- **Be patient.** Some of these experiments may take a few days to work. But you won't get bored! Take a look at your experiment every day while you're waiting, and notice anything that has changed.

- **Be curious.** You may not understand why something happened in every experiment you do, but don't worry about it. The more science experiments you try, the more they will make sense to you. Just have fun!

So grab your lab coat and let's get started!

Dear Mom & Dad,

Maybe science wasn't your best or favorite subject in school. Maybe you're not sure how to make it interesting for your child. That's okay. That's why this book was written.

Many skills are reinforced by exploring science. Your child will practice measuring, telling time, reading, and following directions. These experiments make it fun—so don't feel like you will be forcing your child to do homework-type activities on a weekend. Once she makes her volcano erupt or builds her own camera, you'll find your child is eagerly awaiting her next opportunity to be a scientist.

Each experiment contains simple instructions and easy-to-follow illustrations. There are also explanations of what should happen and how it happens, so you can answer all those inevitable "why" questions.

We rate each experiment for level of ease, but don't discourage your child from doing an experiment that is marked older than her years. If you are there to help her, she should be able to follow the steps. And it is okay if she doesn't understand the scientific principles of the why and how; she may just enjoy watching the results.

So grab your child, choose an experiment, and discover some super science together!

About This Book

Before you get started, read this page.

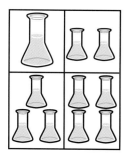

Beaker Ratings

Each experiment has one to four beakers in the upper right corner. They let you know if an experiment is easy or a little more challenging. One beaker is the easiest. If you find an experiment that sounds fun but seems like it might be difficult, try it anyway, as long as a grown-up helps you.

Pocketwatches

If you see this little watch at the top of an experiment, that means it takes a little while before you see the results of your experiment. It could take a few hours, a few days, or even a few weeks. But don't be discouraged! It's worth the wait.

Stop Signs

If you see a stop sign next to a step in any of these experiments, it means that step is a little difficult and you definitely need a grown-up's help. It might include using an oven, a knife, or some other hard-to-handle object.

Science Sleuth

Scattered throughout the book, you'll find "Science Sleuth" pages. These pages investigate certain scientific ideas. With a grown-up's help, read through the pages to learn about different topics, and then try some of the *"Try this"* suggestions at the end of each article.

Science Magic

Some of the experiments in this book are also magic tricks! You'll find them on pages that have the words *Science Magic* at the top. When you learn how to do all these tricks, try putting on a magic show for your friends.

The Human Body

You are made up of millions of cells that work together. Every day your heart must pump and your lungs must breathe. Every day you eat, sleep, breathe, play, and think. But you can do those things only when all your body parts talk to each other and work with each other. When you study your body, you are studying the science of anatomy.

The Amazing Egg I

Turn an egg into a giant rubbery ball to show how your cells get food.

You'll need:

1 uncooked egg in its shell
jar with a lid
white vinegar
cloth measuring tape

1. Wrap the measuring tape around the middle of the egg. Write down that measurement.

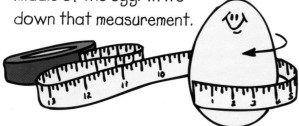

2. Place the egg inside the jar. Make sure it does not crack.

3. Pour enough vinegar into the jar to cover the egg. Screw on the lid.

4. Leave the egg in the jar for three days. Every once in awhile, check on the egg. Notice how it is changing.

5. After three days, carefully take the egg out of the jar. Measure around the middle of the egg again.*

What happens? When you put the egg in the vinegar, you see bubbles. After three days the shell of the egg is gone. The egg has gotten bigger.

Why? The eggshell is made of limestone. When the acid in the vinegar touches the limestone, there is a *chemical reaction*. The shell breaks down during this reaction creating gases including carbon dioxide, which causes the bubbles you see.

Vinegar has water in it. The water moves through teeny, tiny holes in the egg's membrane. That process is called *osmosis*. As more water goes inside the egg, it gets bigger. This is the same way that nutrients move into your body's cells.

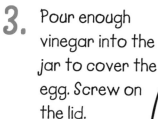

Save this egg for the Amazing Egg II Experiment on the next page.

The Amazing Egg II

Try shrinking the Amazing Egg down to size (or smaller)!

You'll need:

The Amazing Egg (from the previous experiment)
jar with a lid
corn syrup

1. Pour the corn syrup into the jar until it is three inches deep. Gently place the egg in the jar. Screw on the lid.

3"

November

2. Leave the egg in the jar for three days. Check the egg every once in awhile. What does it look like? After three days, carefully take the egg out of the jar. Measure around the middle of the egg.

What happens? The egg shrinks and wrinkles up. It becomes very small and rubbery.

Why? The water molecules inside the egg move through the egg's *membrane* into the corn syrup. The corn syrup does not move into the egg because its *molecules* are too big to fit through the tiny holes in the membrane. Particles move in and out of your body's cells in this way.

Science Sleuth—Cells

Your body is made up of millions of little *cells.* So are plants and dogs and insects and fish. All living things are made of cells.

A cell has three parts. The *membrane* is a thin layer around the cell. It keeps stuff inside. It is kind of like the skin of the cell.

The *nucleus* is like the brain of the cell. It tells the cell what to do and how to act. Some cells have more than one nucleus.

In between the nucleus and the membrane is *cytoplasm.* Cytoplasm looks like jelly.

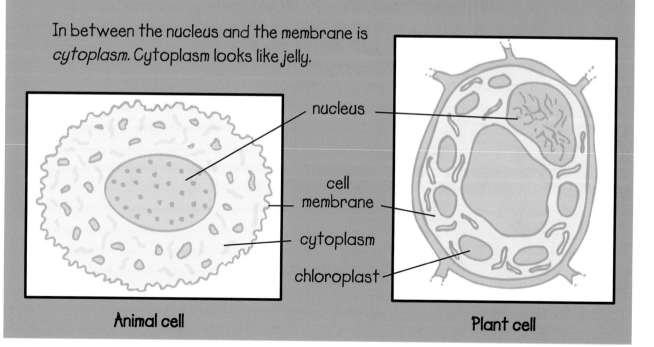

nucleus

cell membrane

cytoplasm

chloroplast

Animal cell

Plant cell

DNA

Cytoplasm contains the things a cell needs to live—food, minerals, and water.

Your cells move oxygen through your body. They make energy for you. They talk to one another so your body can move, eat, and breathe. And they get rid of the things in your body that you don't need.

What makes a blood cell different from a skin cell? *DNA*. DNA is a chemical in the nucleus. It holds the cell's code. It tells the cell what it will be made of, what it will look like, and how it will act. Every person's DNA is different. That's why you are different from everyone else —your cells' DNA is different from your friend's DNA.

 Try this:
- Think about what your DNA says about you. Make a list of all the things about you that you think were decided by your DNA. Now make a list for Mom or Dad. How are your lists the same or different?
- Make a model of a human cell. Find things around the house that you can use to make a nucleus, cytoplasm, and a membrane. Do they look like a cell when you put them together?
- Pretend you are a blood cell. What do you think your nucleus would tell you to do? Try being a skin cell and a brain cell, too.

Dancing Rice

Can you "see" sound?

You'll need:

plastic bowl or coffee can
rubber band
sheet of plastic wrap, a little bigger than
    the top of the can or bowl
spoon
spoonful of uncooked rice
tape

1. Stretch the plastic wrap over the top of the bowl. Wrap the rubber band around it to keep it secure. Tape the edges of the plastic to the bowl to keep the plastic tightly in place.

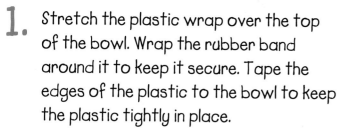

2. Sprinkle some rice on top of the *drum*. Use the spoon to tap the side or top of the *drum*. What happens to the rice?

What happens? The rice jumps around.

Why? When you tap the bowl, the movement makes the plastic *vibrate*. As these vibrations move across the plastic wrap, they make the rice move, too.

Every sound that you hear is made by vibrations. When you sing or talk or cough or laugh, air is pushed over your vocal cords. The vocal cords vibrate (or shake) like the plastic in this experiment and that makes sound.

Homemade Stethoscope

*Track your heart rate and
see how it changes as you move.*

You'll need

3-foot-long piece of rubber tubing
2 funnels (or have an adult cut off the
   tops of two plastic soda bottles)
masking tape
watch with a second hand

1. Place one funnel into the end of the tube. Wrap masking tape around the tube tightly to keep the funnel in place. Do this again with the second funnel and the other end of the tube. You've made your stethoscope.

2. Sit on the couch and relax. Place one funnel over your heart. Put the other funnel over your ear. You should hear your heart beating.

3. Ask a grown-up to time you for 15 seconds. Count the number of heartbeats you hear.

4. With help, multiply the number of heartbeats by 4. This is your *resting heart rate.*

5. Ask your helper to time you again. Run in place for one minute. Then use your stethoscope to check your heart rate again (ask your helper to time you). When you multiply the number of heart beats by 4, you will get your *active heart rate.*

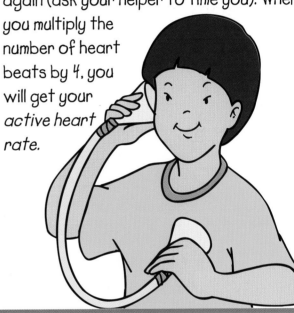

What happens? When you rest, your heart rate is slower than when you are active.

Why? When you exercise, your body burns energy. To burn energy, your cells need more oxygen. Oxygen is brought to your cells through your blood. Your heart pumps the blood so that it moves around your body. When you run, your cells need oxygen right away, so your heart must pump faster.

Your heart is a muscle. While *you* live, it is always working.

Your heart is about the size of your fist. It is found right in the middle of your chest.

The heart is divided into four parts, called *chambers*. Each of the top two parts is called an *atrium*. Each of the bottom two parts is called a *ventricle*.

118, 119, 120!

Your blood travels to your heart. The heart sends it to the lungs to stock up on oxygen and get rid of carbon dioxide. The lungs send the blood back to your heart. Then your heart pumps the blood (full of nutrients and oxygen) to the rest of your body. The heart pumps by *contracting*. A grown-up's heart contracts about 70 times per minute. Your heart contracts about 90 to 120 times each minute.

The heart is divided into four parts called chambers.

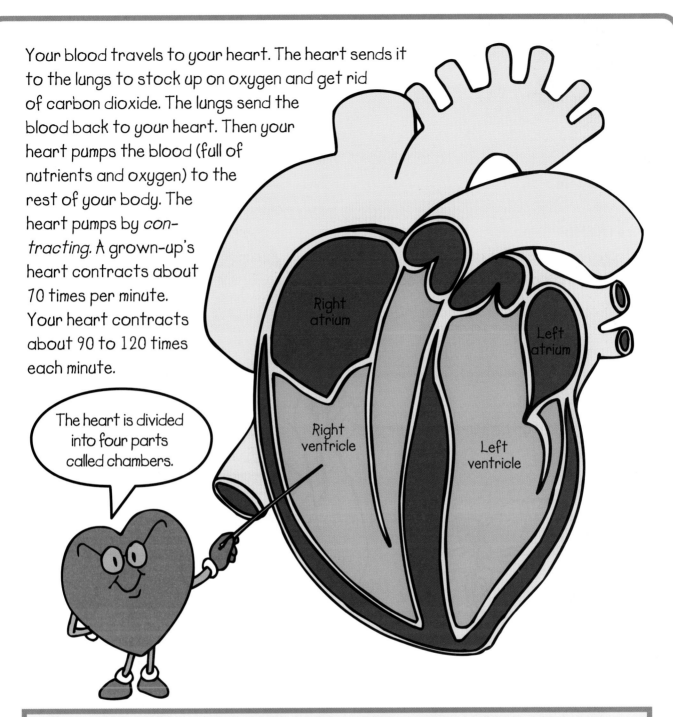

Right atrium

Left atrium

Right ventricle

Left ventricle

 Try this:

* Discover how hard your heart works. Ask a grown-up to time you for one minute. In that minute, make a fist 70 times. Can you imagine doing that for the rest of your life?
* Take your pulse. Lay your arm on a table with your palm facing the ceiling. With the fingers of your other hand, feel around the wrist area below your thumb until you feel your heartbeat. Ask a grown-up to time you for one minute. How many times does your heart beat?

One Eye or Two?

*If both of your eyes do the same thing,
why do we need two instead of one?*

You'll need:

5-inch by 5-inch piece of cardboard
    with holes punched around the edge
shoelace
eye patch, or something to cover
    one eye with

1. Put the eye patch or blindfold over one of your eyes.

2. Ask a grown-up to time you while you thread the shoelace through all the holes. How long did it take? Once you are finished, unthread the shoelace.

3. Take the eye patch off. Ask your grown-up helper to time you while you thread the shoelace through the holes again. How long did it take that time?

What happens? It takes more time to thread the shoelace through the holes when you use only one eye.

Why? Each eye sees things a little bit differently than the other. Our brains combine the information we get from both eyes. This is called *binocular vision*. When you look with two eyes, you give your brain more information than if you use one eye.

A Taste of Outer Space

Why is it harder to drink in outer space?

You'll need:
glass of water
drinking straw
straight-back chair

1. Put the glass of water on the floor near the side of the chair.

2. Lie across the chair so that your stomach is higher than your mouth (see below).

3. Lift the glass and try to take a drink. What happens?

4. Now put the straw in the glass and try to take a sip. What happens?

What happens? It is difficult for you to drink while lying on the chair.

Why? Gravity makes it easy to feed yourself on Earth because it automatically "forces" the food into your mouth and down your throat. There is no gravity in space. When you lie on the chair, you are changing your center of gravity and it is a little harder to get food into your mouth and into your system. When you use a straw, it is a little easier because you are placing pressure on the liquid and forcing it into your mouth. Once the liquid gets into your mouth, the muscles of your throat help it along into your stomach.

No Sweat?!

Find out why you need to sweat.

You'll need:
damp tissue
small fan

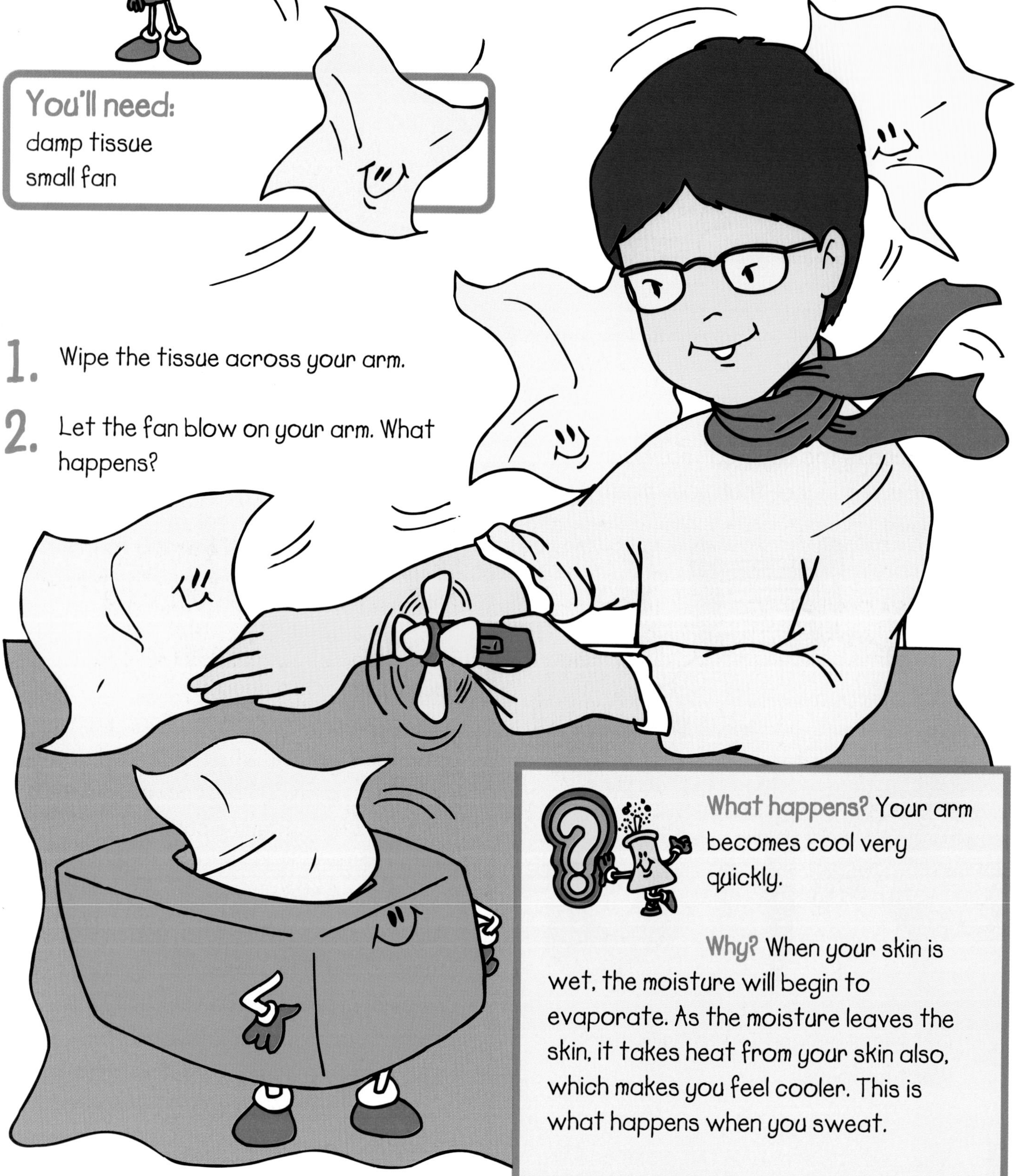

1. Wipe the tissue across your arm.

2. Let the fan blow on your arm. What happens?

What happens? Your arm becomes cool very quickly.

Why? When your skin is wet, the moisture will begin to evaporate. As the moisture leaves the skin, it takes heat from your skin also, which makes you feel cooler. This is what happens when you sweat.

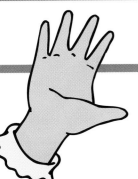

Do some parts of your body depend on other parts to help you move?

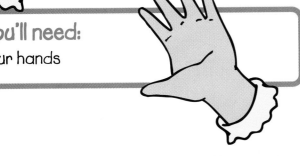

You'll need:
your hands

1. Place the tips of your ring fingers together (starting at your thumb, it is the fourth finger).

2. Fold down your other fingers so the second set of knuckles touches.

3. Try to move your ring fingers apart. Do not slide them up and down! Try moving them backward.

4. Try this again with your other fingers. Can you move any of your other fingers apart?

What happens? It is impossible to move the ring fingers or the middle fingers apart.

Why? The bones in your body are connected to ligaments. *Ligaments* are like little rubber bands that help your bones move around. Your ring fingers and middle fingers are connected to the same ligament. If one of those fingers (and the ligament) is kept from moving, the other one cannot move, either.

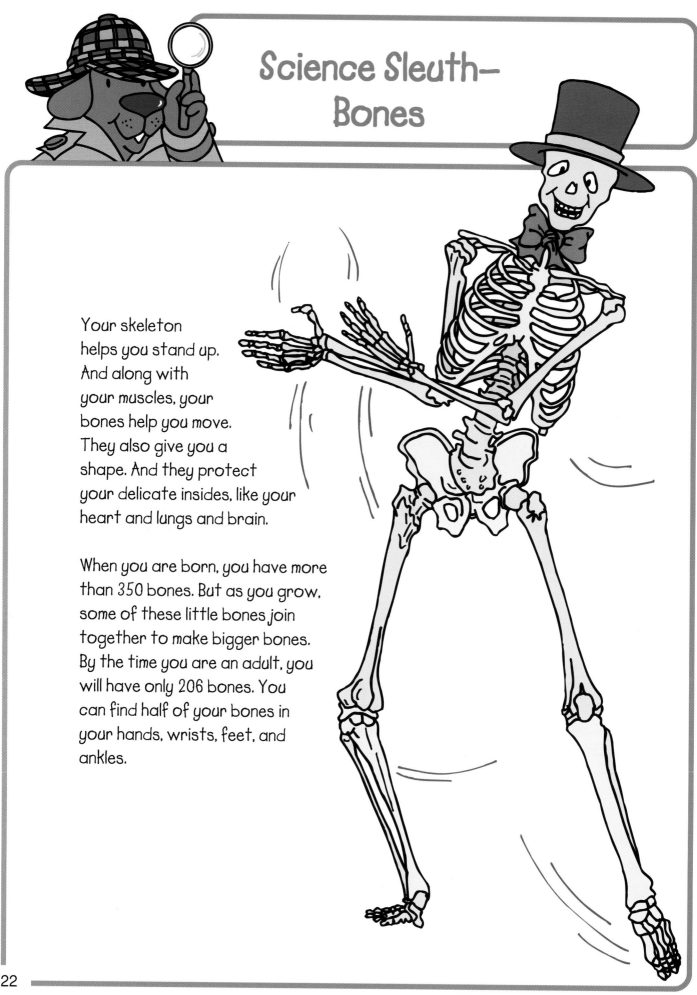

Science Sleuth– Bones

Your skeleton helps you stand up. And along with your muscles, your bones help you move. They also give you a shape. And they protect your delicate insides, like your heart and lungs and brain.

When you are born, you have more than 350 bones. But as you grow, some of these little bones join together to make bigger bones. By the time you are an adult, you will have only 206 bones. You can find half of your bones in your hands, wrists, feet, and ankles.

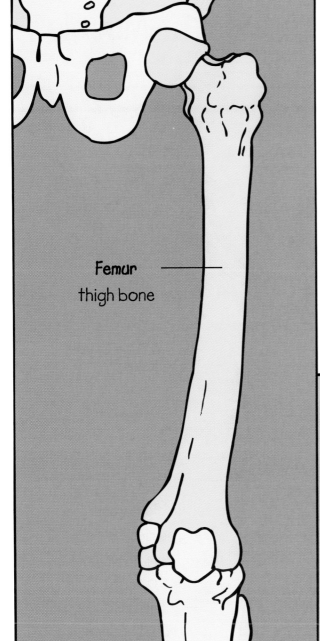

Femur
thigh bone

The biggest bone in your body is your thigh bone, which runs from your hip to your knee. The smallest bone is the stirrup, a tiny bone in your ear, which is only $^7/_{100}$ inch long!

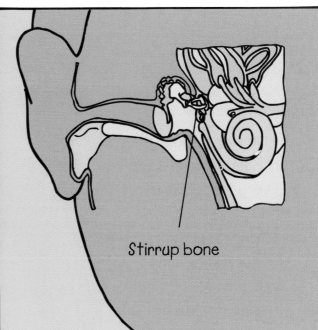

Stirrup bone

 Try this:

- Explore what your bones do for you. Pretend you don't have a skeleton. Show how that would change how you eat, walk, or ride your bike.
- Find out what happens when you break a bone. The next time you go to the doctor, ask her how a cast fixes it.

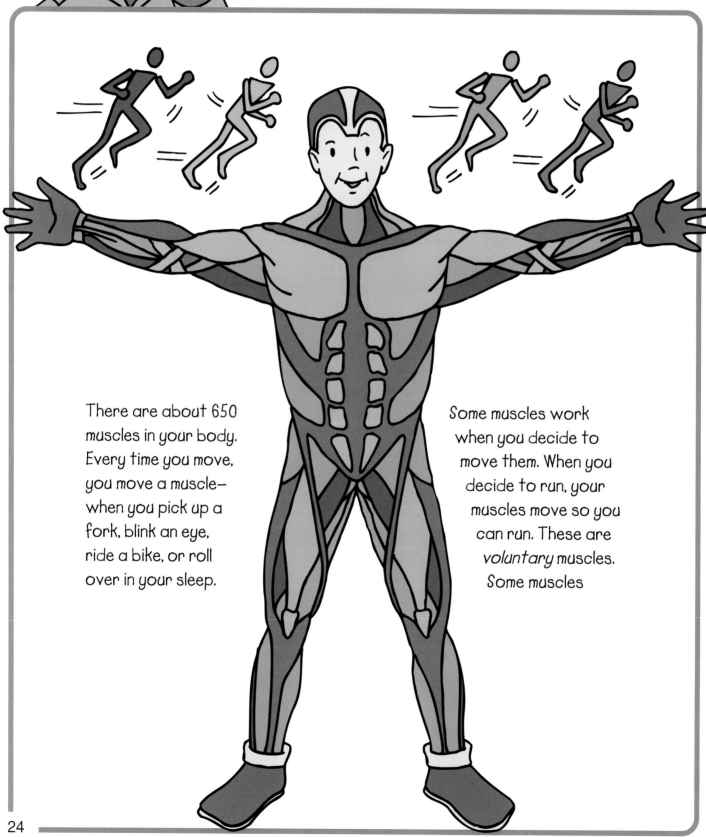

There are about 650 muscles in your body. Every time you move, you move a muscle—when you pick up a fork, blink an eye, ride a bike, or roll over in your sleep.

Some muscles work when *you* decide to move them. When *you* decide to run, your muscles move so you can run. These are *voluntary* muscles. Some muscles

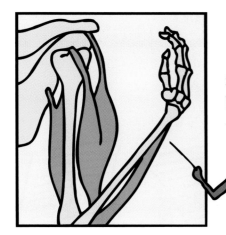

move automatically, like when your heart pumps blood, or muscles around your intestines contract to digest food. These are *involuntary* muscles.

Muscles are connected to the brain by nerves. Nerves are like micro-scopic electrical wires flowing through your body. When you want to write a letter, your brain sends a message through the nerves to the muscles in your hand to pick up a pencil and start writing.

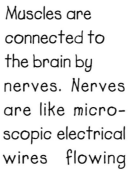

A muscle *contracts*, or tightens, to move. Muscles are attached to *bones*. When a muscle moves, so does the bone that is attached to it. Muscles are always attached to bones, except in your face. In your face, there are 30 muscles. When they contract, they move the skin on your face.

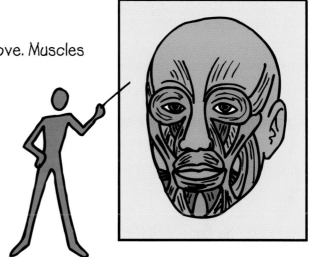

 Try this:
- Feel your muscles. Make a fist. Feel the muscle in the lower half of your arm. Now flex your right arm like a muscleman. Feel the muscle in that arm. How does it feel when you stop flexing?

Collecting Thumbprints

Are you the only person with YOUR thumbprint?

You'll need:

number 2 pencil
clean sheet of paper
transparent tape
plain, white 3-inch by 5-inch index cards

1. Rub the pencil point back and forth on the clean piece of paper. Do it many times until there is pencil-lead dust on the page.

2. Press your thumb into the dust. Ask a grown-up to place the sticky side of a piece of transparent tape on your thumb.

3. Remove the tape. Stick the piece of tape to the index card. Write your name under the thumbprint.

4. Wash your hands. Repeat Steps 1 through 3 on other family members and friends to make a collection of thumbprints.

-April-

-Maureen-

-Daddy-

-Lizzie-

-Chelsea-

-Grandpa-

-Thomas-

-Mom-

-Grandma-

What happens? The tiny ridges in your thumb pick up some of the pencil lead. The valleys between the ridges do not. When you press the tape against your thumb, the ridge pattern transfers from your thumb to the tape. When you collect other thumbprints, you see that no two thumbprints are alike.

Why? Your thumbprint is caused by the *friction ridges* on your thumb. You have friction ridges all over your hands and feet. These ridges make it easier for you to pick things up and to walk in your bare feet. If your hands were completely smooth, objects would just slip out of your hands.

Every person in the world has a different thumbprint. Even identical twins have different thumbprints. Your thumbprint stays the same your whole life, no matter how you grow and change. If you cut the skin on your thumb, it will grow back in the exact same pattern. Police officers use thumbprints to find criminals, solve crimes, and find lost children.

Science Sleuth–Amazing Human Body Facts

Answer TRUE or FALSE to the questions below. Answers are on page 150.

A. Your small intestines are 5 feet long and the large intestines are 20 feet long.

B. Old skin cells are eventually shed from your body. In your lifetime, you will shed about 40 pounds of skin.

C. Your normal body temperature is 98.6°.

D. It takes two muscles to smile.

E. In the 1800s, people believed you could tell what a person was like by feeling the bulges on his head.

F. The blood in your veins is blue because of oxygen.

G. You have 5 million hairs on your body.

H. Each eyelash lasts about four years.

I. Brain cells last your whole lifetime.

J. The smallest cells in your body are the brain cells.

K. The dust around your house is made up mostly of dead skin cells.

Fill in the blank with the correct answer. Answers are on page 150.

1. When you sneeze, air rushes out of your nose at _____ miles per hour!

2. Each day, you blink your eyes about _____ times!

3. Each day, your heart beats about _____ times!

4. There are about _____ hairs on your head.

5. About _____ of your body is made of water!

6. A baby has about _____ cells in his body. An adult has about _____.

7. Your brain weighs ___% of your body weight, and uses ___% of your body's energy.

8. You have about _____ miles of blood vessels in your body.

9. It can take _____ for a meal to pass through your digestive system.

10. A woman in England sneezed continuously for _____ days.

11. A man in Iowa hiccupped every 1½ seconds for more than_____ years!

12. There are more red blood cells in your body than any other cell—we each have about _____.

 Try this:
- Try using the facts on these pages to make your own game about the human body.

Air

You may not be able to see air, but it's there. It helps living things breathe, helps birds and airplanes fly, helps you hear, and helps create certain kinds of energy. Every living thing needs air.

Soaring Airplanes

Find out how airplanes fly.

You'll need:
a few sheets of $8\frac{1}{2}$-inch by
   11-inch paper
paper clip
ruler

1. Fold one piece of paper in half length-wise. Open it again (see at right).

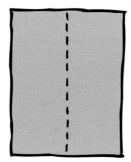

2. Fold down each of the top two corners to make them meet in the middle. Now fold down the top triangle, as shown below.

3. Fold up the point of the triangle so it is about an inch long. The paper will still have a rectangle shape.

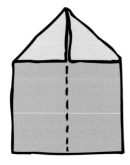

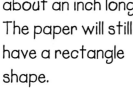

4. Fold the top corners of the rectangle so they meet in the center. They will be on top of the little triangle.

5. Fold down the folded edges of the plane again so they meet in the middle.

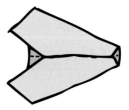

6. Fold the plane in half lengthwise, along the center line. There! You've made a paper airplane!

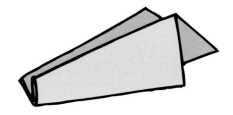

How to fly the plane:

The narrower end is the front. Hold the plane as shown. After flying it a few times, attach a paper clip just under the nose. Does it fly better with the paper clip? What happens if you move the paper clip to another part of the plane?

Doing tricks:

A *Barrel Roll*—Bend one tailpiece up about an inch. Bend the other tailpiece down about an inch. Now fly the plane. A *Loop-the-Loop*—Bend both tailpieces down. If you want the plane to come right back to you, try aiming upward when you throw.

What happens? Your airplane flew, of course!

Why? Airplanes don't fly exactly like birds—when was the last time you saw a plane flap its wings up and down?—but they do use a lot of the same forces when they fly. The wings of an airplane are usually rounded at the front and narrower at the back, like a bird's wings. The curve makes the air above the wing move faster than the air below the wing. This lifts the plane into the air. When you bend your plane's tail in different directions, you change the way the air moves around your paper plane. That's what makes it do tricks.

Speed is necessary to keep your plane in the air. A paper airplane does not have a motor to keep it moving fast, so when it loses speed, it won't fly anymore.

Beaker Bonus: Leonardo da Vinci drew a design for a flying machine almost 500 years before helicopters and airplanes were invented!

Make a Grab for It

Air magically "lifts" a marble.

You'll need:

2 pieces of cardboard (about 8
    inches long and 1 inch wide)
1-inch length of a small wooden rod
small deflated balloon
tape
colored paper
a few marbles

To prepare:

1. Blow a little air into the balloon and tie the end.

2. Place the balloon between the two pieces of cardboard, as shown below. Tape the balloon to the cardboard, leaving about an inch and a half of space from one end of the cardboard strips.

3. Tape the wooden rod inside the pieces of cardboard, as shown below.

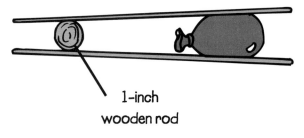

1-inch
wooden rod

4. Wrap colored paper around the cardboard pieces to hide the balloon and rod.

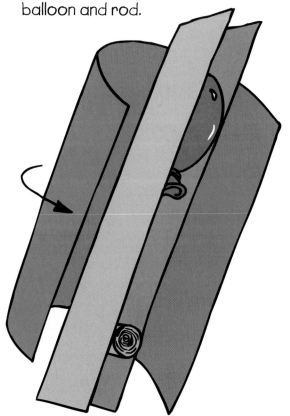

To do the trick:

1. Hold the grabber so the end with the balloon is facing down. Show the audience how you can easily pick up a marble: Squeeze the balloon end of the grabber together to grab the marble.

2. Ask a volunteer to do the same thing. As you hand her the grabber, turn it so she will be holding the rod side down. No matter how much she tries, she will not be able to pick up a marble!

 **What happens?** When you squeeze the balloon end of the grabber, you can pick up a marble. When an audience member tries to pick up a marble with the wooden-rod end, she can't do it.

Why? When the rod end is squeezed, it does not move. The rod keeps the cardboard strips from moving together. When you squeeze the balloon end together, the air inside the balloon is compressed, and the cardboard strips can move closer together. When the strips move together, they are working like a *lever*.

Science Sleuth—Flight

People learned how to make airplanes by studying how birds fly. Birds can fly because of the air that flows over their wings.

A bird's wing is curved on the top and flat on the bottom, like this:

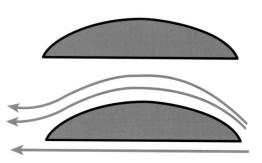

When a bird flaps its wings, air rushes over and under the wings. Because the top of each wing curves, the air on top has farther to go than the air on the bottom:

The air on top must move faster than the air on the bottom if it wants to move over the wing in the same amount of time. The faster air moves, the less pressure it has. So there is more pressure under the wing, and less pressure on top. When the air presses more on the bottom of the wing, it pushes the wing (and the bird) up.

While airplanes do not flap their wings up and down, they do have wings that are curved on the top and flat on the bottom. Air pressure works the same way to make planes fly.

People wanted to fly for thousands of years. They made wings to flap, but that didn't work. Leonardo da Vinci made sketches of flying machines more than 500 years ago, but he never built one that worked.

The first power-driven plane was flown on December 17, 1903, near Kitty Hawk, North Carolina. It was piloted by Orville Wright while his brother Wilbur watched. The plane flew a distance of 120 feet at 30 miles per hour. It flew about 10 feet off the ground! You can now see that plane, *Flyer I*, in the National Air and Space Museum at the Smithsonian Institution in Washington, D.C.

 Try this:
- Make a model airplane with clay. Design the wings so they look just like a real airplane's wings.
- Create a new kind of paper airplane. Using what you know about flight, make a paper airplane unlike any kind you've ever seen before.
- Find out more about the Wright brothers. Draw and write a comic book about their adventures.

Paper Cup Parachutes

How do parachutes work?

You'll need:

14-inch square cut from a plastic
    garbage bag
four 14-inch lengths of string
small paper cup
hole puncher

1. Poke a tiny hole in the center of the plastic.

2. Tie a knot in each corner of the plastic. Tie a length of string above each knot.

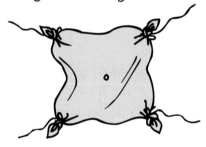

3. **STOP** Use the hole puncher to punch four holes around the top of the paper cup as shown. Tie the loose ends of the strings to the paper cup.

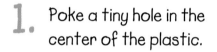

4. Go outside. Toss your parachute into the air. What happens? Toss your parachute again, as high as you can. What happens?

5. Stuff the parachute inside the cup. Toss the cup in the air. What happens?

What happens? When you throw the parachute in the air, it spreads out. When you stuff the parachute inside the cup, it can't open and it falls faster.

Why? When air gets under the parachute, the parachute opens and friction is created. When there is friction, objects cannot move as fast. Without a parachute, the cup falls faster because there is less friction to slow its fall.

Balloon Rocket

What makes a rocket shoot upward into the air?

You'll need:

6 feet of string
2 chairs
drinking straw
long balloon
masking tape

4. Once the balloon is taped to the straw, let go of it. What happens?

1. Tie the string to the top of one chair. Thread the string through the straw. Tie the other end of the string to the other chair.

Air pushes out

Balloon zooms forward

2. Move the chairs far enough apart so the string is pulled tight.

What happens? The balloon and straw move along the string, away from the balloon opening.

Why? When you blow the balloon up, you put air inside it. The skin of the balloon presses in on that air. When you let go of the balloon, the force of the skin pushes the air out the opening. The force of the air pushes the balloon in the other direction. When a real rocket is launched, its fuel lights and "explodes" out of the bottom. This also creates a force that pushes the rocket up into the sky.

3. Blow up the balloon. Pinch the ends together so the air can't get out. While you hold the balloon shut, have someone tape the balloon to the straw, as shown below.

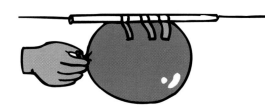

Science Sleuth— Rockets

The very first rockets were probably built in the 1200s in China. They were very small, and for hundreds of years were used as fireworks and weapons.

A rocket has some kind of fuel inside it. When the fuel mixes with the oxygen in the air, there is an explosion. The explosion creates a force that pushes downward. That push propels the rocket forward through the air.

But how do we send rockets into space? There is no oxygen there, so there is no way to burn the fuel.

A man named Robert Goddard made a rocket that used gasoline and liquid oxygen to cause the explosion. This was in 1926. His first rocket traveled up 184 feet at 60 miles per hour. The whole flight took only 2.5 seconds. But his idea is used today in space rockets, including space shuttles.

A space shuttle is made up of four parts. There are two booster rockets, the main fuel tank, and the orbiter. The orbiter is the planelike piece where the shuttle's crew sits. There are four orbiters—*Discovery*, *Columbia*, *Atlantis*, and *Endeavour*.

Two minutes after the launch, the booster rockets fall off and parachute into the ocean. Ships bring them back to the Kennedy Space Center to get them ready for the next launch.

Eight minutes after the launch, the main fuel tank falls off and breaks up into little pieces. It is not used again.

The orbiter moves at a speed of 17,000 miles per hour! It takes only ten minutes for it to zoom over the United States.

The orbiter is a rocket while it is taking off and while it is in space. On its way back to Earth, though, it is like a glider, and looks like a plane when it is landing.

 Try this:

- Watch the next space shuttle launch on television.
- Borrow a book about space shuttles from the library.
- Make a cardboard rocket and figure out how to launch it WITHOUT any kind of explosion.

Bottled Eggs

Is it possible to squeeze an egg into a soda bottle?

You'll need:

hard-boiled egg
scrap of paper wadded-up
long matches
empty glass bottle with a narrow neck

1. Peel the shell off the egg. Place the narrow side of the egg on top of the bottle. What happens?

2. Take the egg off the bottle. Place the paper inside the bottle. (STOP) Ask a grown-up to light the scrap paper using a long match. Place the narrow end of the egg on top of the bottle right away. What happens?

3. Try to get the egg back out of the bottle. Can you do it? If not, try blowing into the bottle. See what happens.

What happens? The egg falls into the bottle when you burn the scrap paper inside. When you blow into the bottle, it pops out.

Why? When you first try to get the egg in the bottle, the air pressure inside the bottle is the same as the air pressure outside the bottle. When you set fire to the scrap paper inside the bottle, the air inside the bottle gets hotter. The molecules start moving around more. They are very excited, and they want to get out of the jar. But they can't, because the egg is blocking their way. As the air gets hotter and the molecules move faster, the air pressure is building inside the bottle. The air pressure becomes so great that it pushes the egg upward a few times.

But at the same time, when you burn that piece of paper, you are burning oxygen. The oxygen gradually becomes a solid. The air pressure inside the bottle then starts to decrease. As it decreases, there is not enough air pressure inside the bottle to keep the egg from falling into the bottle.

Blow Hard

Does air take up space?

You'll need:

7-inch balloon

glass soda bottle (6-ounce to
10-ounce size)

straw

ball of clay (about the size of a walnut)

masking tape

scissors

1.  Use the scissors to cut the lip off the balloon. Pull the balloon over the straw until it covers 1/2 inch of the straw. Wrap tape around the edge of the balloon so it is attached to the straw as shown.

2. Place the straw and balloon inside the bottle as shown. Press the clay around the straw and the mouth of the bottle to make it airtight.

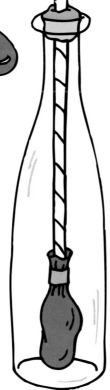

3. Blow into the straw. Try to inflate the balloon.

 **What happens?** You can only inflate the balloon a tiny bit no matter how much you blow.

Why? When you put the balloon in the bottle, the bottle is not really empty. It is filled with air. If you blow the balloon up, it will get bigger. To make room for the balloon, you need to get rid of some of the air in the bottle. But there is no place for the air to go, because you have blocked the opening in the bottle.

41

"Marble-ous" Magic

Can you make a marble move without touching it?

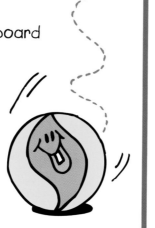

You'll need:

cardboard box
small piece of cardboard
glue
tape
colored paper
scissors
2 small plastic bags
straw
large cloth
marble

To prepare:

1. Cut a small hole (big enough for the marble to sit in) in the center of the small piece of cardboard. Glue this piece of cardboard to the top of the box.

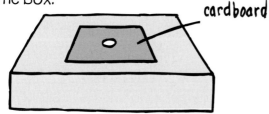

cardboard

2. Use colored paper to decorate the box so it looks magical.

3. Lay the two plastic bags flat on a tabletop. Tape the openings of the bags closed, except for a small opening at the center of each.

small opening

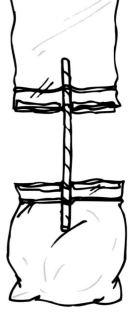

4. Push the straw into the opening of one bag. Blow into the straw so the bag inflates. Put the other bag on the other end of the straw.

5. Put the bags on the table where you will be doing the trick. Cover them with a cloth so they are hidden.

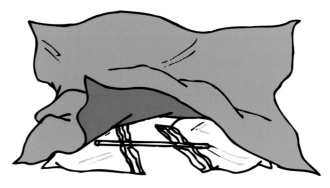

To do the trick:

1. Put the box on top of the deflated bag. Place the marble on top of the box.

2. Tell the audience that you will move the marble with your mind. Concentrate hard on the marble, and secretly press down on the other bag.

What happens? The box shakes, and the marble rolls off.

Why? When you press down on the inflated plastic bag, the air in that bag pushes through the straw and into the other bag. As the air pushes the plastic bag up and outward, the box is also pushed up, causing the marble to roll off. These bags are an example of a *pneumatic machine* (new MAT tic mah SHEEN).

Plastic Kite

How does a kite fly?

You'll need:

2 wood strips, each 22 inches long
    and 1/8 inch wide
25-inch by 22-inch sheet of heavy plastic
pen
tape
small metal O-ring (you can get one at the
    hardware store)
kite line (at least 90 feet)
scissors
pliers
stiff wire
ruler

1. Ask a grown-up to draw the kite design below on the plastic sheet (be sure to enlarge the size!). 🛑 Cut out the design.

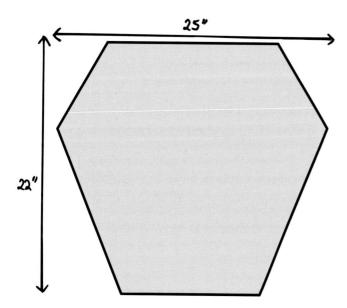

25"

22"

2. Tape the wood strips to the kite at the points marked here. Put some strips of tape along the outermost corners of the kite. Poke a hole through each of the pieces of tape.

3. 🛑 With help, measure a 34-inch length of kite line. Cut it. Thread and tie each end of the length of kite line through one of the corner holes.

4. Pull the kite line through the O-ring. Pass the loop back over the ring and through itself. Pull the line to make sure it is secure around the ring.

5. 🛑 Ask a grown-up to use the pliers to bend the stiff wire as shown below. This will be the spool for the line. Wrap tape around the ends and the handle to cover sharp edges. Wrap at least 90 feet of line around the spool. Tie the other end of the line to the O-ring.

How to fly a kite:

1. Find an open space outside. Stay away from buildings, electric lines, and trees. An open field or the beach is a great place.

2. Make sure it is not raining or lightning. There should be a light wind.

3. Ask a grown-up to hold the kite and face the wind. You hold the kite spool. Stand about ten feet away from your helper, with your back to the wind.

4. When your helper releases the kite into the air, unspool the line a little.

5. If the kite begins to come down, try pulling on the line a little. If your kite starts to move around wildly, let some of the line out until it straightens itself.

What happens? Your kite does not fly straight up and down. It flies at an angle.

Why? When the wind hits the kite, the kite pushes the wind downward. As the wind flows down, the kite is pushed up.

Wacky Wand

Magically guard yourself against "pushovers."

You'll need:

5-foot-long broomstick
colored paper
paint
paintbrush
glue
scissors

To do the trick:

1. Tell the audience that your super-sized wand gives you extra-super strength.

2. Have a member of the audience hold one end of the wand while you hold the other. Ask your volunteer to try to push you over with the wand.

3. Before your volunteer starts pushing, lift your end of the wand over your head.

To prepare:

1. Paint your broomstick to look like a magic wand—white on the ends and black in the middle. Paint or use the colored paper and glue to make magical symbols on the wand.

What happens? Your volunteer cannot push you over. You remain standing.

Why? If you hold the wand straight in front of you when the volunteer pushes, the force on the wand will push you also. But when you lift up your end of the wand, the force is trying to push you up <u>and</u> back. This means less of the total force is pushing you backward, so you can remain standing straight.

Kazoo

Why do kazoos make sounds?

You'll need:

toilet-tissue or paper-towel tube
small, square piece of waxed paper
rubber band
pencil

1. Place the waxed paper over one end of the cardboard tube.

2. Wrap a rubber band around the waxed paper to keep it in place.

3. Use the pencil to poke a small hole on the side of the tube near the unwrapped end.

4. Hold the unwrapped end of the kazoo to your mouth as shown. Hum through the end of the kazoo. Feel the other end of the kazoo while you hum. What happens?

5. Cover the tiny hole with your finger and blow air into the kazoo.

What happens? You feel the vibrations of your hums when you put your hand on the other end of the kazoo. When you cover the tiny airhole, the sound is very low and muffled.

Why? When something *vibrates*, it usually makes a sound. When you blow air into the kazoo, the air starts to vibrate, and it makes the kazoo vibrate also, which makes a sound.

Rubber-Band Music

Can you make different sounds using rubber bands?

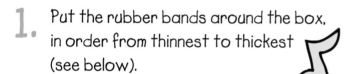

You'll need:

shallow cake pan
rubber bands that are different
    sizes and widths
ruler

1. Put the rubber bands around the box, in order from thinnest to thickest (see below).

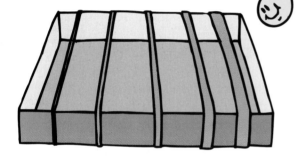

2. Pluck the rubber bands. How do they sound?

3. Slide the ruler under the rubber bands so it is in the center of the box, as shown below. Now pluck the rubber bands. How do they sound?

4. Now slide the ruler a little bit to the right or left. Pluck each rubber band, first on its long side, and then on its short side. How does each sound?

What happens? The rubber bands sound different after you place the ruler under them. And when you move the ruler to the side and pluck each side of the rubber bands, each side will make a different sound.

Why? When you place the ruler under the rubber bands, it touches part of each rubber band. When it does, those sections of the rubber bands don't *vibrate*, so there is less space on each rubber band for the vibrations. This changes the sound.

When you move the ruler more to one side, it creates a short side and a long side on each rubber band. On the long side, vibrations have to travel farther along the band, so they travel slower, making a lower sound. On the short side, vibrations move faster, making the shorter side vibrate more, so the sound is higher.

Bottle Music

How can you make music with a few glass bottles?

You'll need:
5 small, narrow-mouthed glass bottles
  (they should all be exactly the same)
water

1. Put a different amount of water in each bottle.

2. Place your lower lip up against one of the bottle's openings. Blow gently. Move your lips around until you make a sound. Do this with all the bottles.

What happens? Each bottle makes a different sound. *(Can you perform a tune on your musical bottles?)*

Why? When you blow in the opening of the bottle, you make sound waves. You do this by making the air inside the bottle vibrate. All the bottles have a different amount of air in them, depending on how much water you put inside them. The *pitch* of the sound each bottle makes depends on how fast the air is vibrating. The bottles with less water and more air will sound deeper and lower because there are slower vibrations. The bottles with more water and less air will sound higher because there are faster vibrations.

Rabbit Hole

How can you make a rabbit pop out of a box?

You'll need:

cardboard box
scissors
plastic tubing
2 deflated balloons
rubber bands
markers
cardboard
stiff paper
tape

To prepare:

1. 🛑 Cut a small hole in the back of the cardboard box. Cut a small hole in top of the box.

2. Push one end of the tubing through the hole in the back and then up through the hole on top.

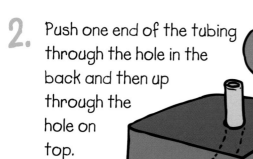

3. Place one deflated balloon over the end of the tube that is on top of the box. Wrap a rubber band around the neck of the balloon to keep it in place. Blow up the second balloon. Put it over the other end of the tube. Wrap a rubber band around the neck of that balloon, also.

4. Draw a bunny like the one below on the piece of cardboard. 🛑 Cut it out. Tape the bunny to the top of the balloon that is on top of the box.

5. Take a piece of stiff paper. Tape the ends together to make a cylinder. Place the cylinder over the balloon and bunny, so they are hidden. Tape the cylinder to the box. Decorate the box and paper cylinder to make them look magical.

1. Tell the audience that you would like them to meet your pet rabbit, but he is shy. Ask them to call your rabbit, very loudly.

2. While your audience is calling to the rabbit, slowly press on the balloon at the back of the box to make the rabbit rise.

What happens? The rabbit rises out of the cylinder.

Why? When you attach your balloons to the tube, you make a kind of *pneumatic machine* (new MAT tic mah SHEEN). As you press on the inflated balloon, the air inside the balloon is pushed forward. It moves through the tube and into the deflated balloon. When the air moves into the deflated balloon, the balloon stretches outward to make room for the air molecules. As more air moves into the balloon, it gets bigger. As it gets bigger and moves outward, the rabbit moves upward.

Pinwheel

What makes a pinwheel turn?

You'll need:

8-inch square piece of construction paper
long, straight pin
bead
chopstick
scissors
pencil

1. Divide the square of paper by drawing two lines from corner to corner, as shown here.

4. (STOP) When you've gathered all four corners in the middle, ask a grown-up to push the pin through them.

5. Place the bead on the back end of the pin. (STOP) Ask a grown-up to push the pin into the end of the chopstick.

6. Blow on the pinwheel or take it outside when there is a breeze.

2. (STOP) With help, cut along the lines from each corner almost to the center. Be sure the paper stays in one piece!

3. The paper is now divided into four triangles. Bend the right corner of each triangle toward the center.

What happens? The pinwheel turns in the breeze.

Why? When the wind blows, air molecules are being pushed along. When these moving molecules bump into objects that are not very heavy, they push those objects in the same direction that they are moving. When the wind hits the pinwheel, the air molecules push the pinwheel in the direction that they are moving.

Light

You may not think about sunlight much, but it is important to everything on the Earth. It keeps us warm and makes the Earth livable. It helps plants make food, and those plants are eaten by animals. We can tell time and cook with it. It makes rainbows, and helps cameras and kaleidoscopes work. If it weren't for the Sun's energy, there would be nothing on the Earth!

Night Vision

How much can you see in the dark?

You'll need:

big bunch of different-colored socks that have not been sorted

some shirts that belong to you, Mom, Dad, your brother, or your sister

1. Once it is dark outside, go into a room (with a grown-up helper) and close the door. Close the blinds or shades so that only a little bit of light comes into the room. Turn out the lights.

2. Look around the room. What can you see? How close do you have to get to something to see it? Is it easier to see objects that are closer to the window?

3. Sort the socks in the dark. Make a pile of white ones, a pile of red ones, a pile of blue ones, and a pile for each of the other colors.

4. Ask your helper to stand on the other side of the room and hold up the shirts one at a time. Can you tell whom the shirt belongs to right away?

5. Look around the room again. What can you see now? Is it easier to see in the dark as time passes than it was when you first turned off the lights?

What happened? You probably sorted some of the socks wrong, because you couldn't really see the colors. It was probably very hard to see things, especially from far away. However, as time passed and your eyes adjusted, it probably got easier.

Why? The human eye is not made to see very well in the dark. We really don't need to, since we are usually asleep at night. You *can* see better once you've been in the dark awhile because your *rods* begin to notice patterns of light.

A lot of animals can see as well at night as we see during the day. They are *nocturnal* animals. These are usually animals that hunt for their food at night, or are being hunted. Being able to see in the dark can help them find food, or can help them escape from becoming another animal's food. Nocturnal animals usually have very big eyes (to let more light in) or very big ears (to catch more sound waves).

Rainbow in a Box

Is a rainbow made by rain or the sun?

You'll need:

scissors
shoebox
white paper
clear drinking glass
water

4. Fill the glass with water. Place it in the box, up against the slit. What do you see on the paper?

1. On one end of the shoebox, cut a 1/2-inch slit.

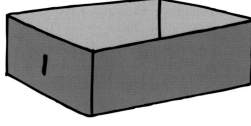

2. Place the paper in the bottom of the box. You may need to ask a grown-up to trim the paper to make it fit.

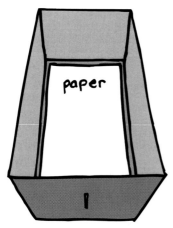

paper

3. Place the box in a window in the morning. Be sure the sun can enter the box through the slit.

What happens? You saw a rainbow on the white paper.

Why? Light travels in waves. The light waves enter the box. When they hit the water, they bend. They spread out and group together according to their wavelengths. Different wavelengths make different colors, which is how a rainbow is made.

Sun Race

Does sunlight affect the way plants grow?

You'll need:

2 same-size shoeboxes with lids
6 cardboard strips that fit inside
    the shoeboxes
scissors
2 sprouting potatoes
tape

1. Cut a hole in the end of one of the shoeboxes. In each box, tape the cardboard strips so they make a maze (see below). Be sure the lids will fit on when you are finished.

2. Place one potato in the box with the hole. It should be put at the end of the box without the hole. Put the other potato in the other box.

3. Put the lids on both boxes. Place both boxes in a sunny spot. Make sure the hole is facing the light.

4. Once a day for two weeks, check your boxes to see how your potatoes are growing.

What happens? The potato in the box with the hole sprouts a stem that grows around the maze to reach the light. The potato in the other box does not sprout any stems.

Why? Plants need light to grow. They will always grow toward the light, as if they want to get as close as possible to it. That is why the potato in the holey box grows around the maze.

Science Sleuth—Cameras

A camera usually has two lenses. You look through one lens when you get ready to take a picture. The second lens is in the front of the camera, and is used to focus the light that is coming into the camera.

There is a mirror inside a camera, and when light comes in the front lens, the mirror reflects the light up to the top lens. This lets you see the object at which you are pointing your camera. When you press the button to take a picture, you are telling the camera to move the mirror up. When this happens, the light hits the film.

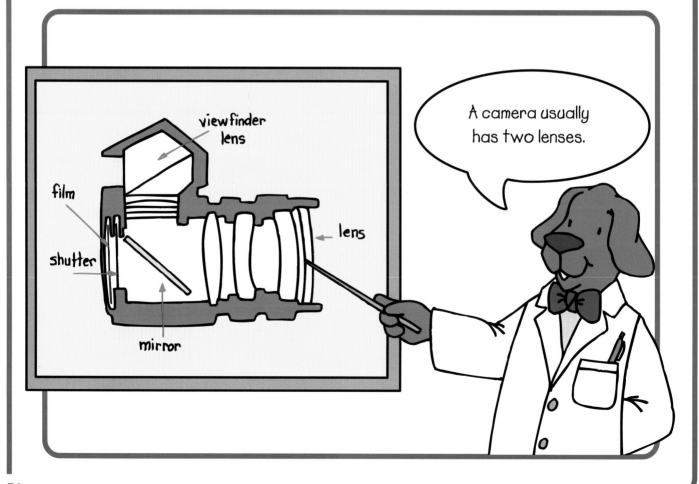

... light comes in the front lens, the mirror reflects the light up to the top lens (viewfinder) ...

When light hits the film, an impression of the object in front of the camera is made on the film. When the film is developed, you have your picture.

 Try this:
- Take several pictures of your house at different times of the day. Notice how the pictures change. How did light affect the pictures?
- Make a storybook and illustrate it with pictures. First write a story. Then take some pictures of things you mention in the story. Paste the pictures into a homemade booklet and write the story below the pictures.
- Start a scrapbook. Take pictures on special occasions that you want to remember. Keep them in a photo album.
- Experiment with your camera. Change the settings when you take pictures. Notice how the pictures look different when you change the settings.

Make Your Own Camera

How does light make a camera work?

You'll need:

black-and-white 126 film cartridge

black tape

1¼-inch by 5¾-inch piece
    of black cardboard

1½-inch by 2¾-inch piece
    of black cardboard

1-inch square piece of aluminum foil

2 rubber bands

needle

pencil

scissors

dime

2. (STOP) Use the needle to poke a tiny hole in the center of the aluminum foil.

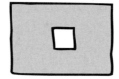

3. Draw a square (less than 1 inch by 1 inch) in the middle of the other piece of cardboard. (STOP) With help, cut the square out. Use the black tape to tape the foil square over the square-shaped opening. Do not cover up the hole in the foil.

1. With help, divide the larger piece of cardboard into four equal sections, as shown. Fold the cardboard along the sections to make a box, like the one shown. Tape the edges of the box together with black tape.

4. Tape the flat piece of cardboard over the opening of the cardboard box you made in Step 1. Put black tape along all the edges between the two pieces of cardboard as shown (this will keep out the light).

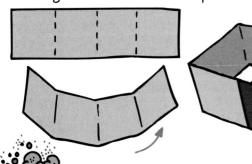

Beaker Bonus: The first camera was made in 1593 in Italy. It was made out of a box with a small hole in it. It was used to help people trace pictures of which they wanted copies.

5. Use the rubber bands to attach the film to the back of the camera.

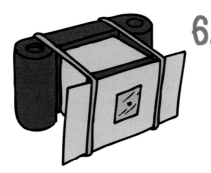

6. Place a small piece of black tape over the hole in the aluminum foil.

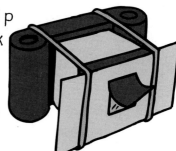

How to take a picture:

1. Ask a grown-up to help you wind the film. Place a dime in the round opening of the cartridge. Wind the film until the number 1 is showing.

2. Point the camera at what you want to photograph. To take a picture, lift the black tape that covers the hole in the foil. Keep the camera perfectly still when you do this. Then cover the pinhole with the tape again.

3. Use the dime to wind the film to your next picture.

4. Repeat Steps 2 and 3 until you have used all the film and you can't wind it any farther.

5. When the roll of film is done, remove the film from the camera and take it to a store to be developed.

What happens? Your camera takes pictures.

Why? All cameras work the same way, whether it is your homemade camera or a fancy one you buy in the store. When light comes through the little pinhole, it "reacts" with the chemicals on your film. When this happens, the film makes a copy of whatever image it sees through the hole.

Beaker Bonus: A company in England owns a camera that is almost 9 feet high, more than 8 feet wide, and 46 feet long!!! And in Japan they sell the "Petal" camera which is circle shaped and is about 1 inch by $1/2$ inch!

Sundial

How can you tell time with the Sun?

You'll need:

small ball of clay
small flowerpot
chopstick
ruler
pencil
watch

1. Press the clay into the bottom of the flowerpot. Push one end of the chopstick into the clay. About three inches of the chopstick should stick up above the top of the pot.

2. When the sun is rising, put the flowerpot outside in a sunny spot. Make a mark on the rim of the flowerpot where the chopstick makes a shadow. Write what time it is next to this mark.

If you could see through the flowerpot, it would look like this.

3. For the rest of the day, mark the spot where the shadow hits the edge of the pot at each hour until the sun sets (at 7 A.M., 8 A.M., 9 A.M., etc.). Be sure to write the time next to each mark.

4. Now you have a sundial! Leave the pot in the same place and you will be able to tell the approximate time of day by using the sun.

What happens? As the day goes by, the shadow moves around the pot. As you mark the time on the rim, you make a clock!

Why? Every day, the Earth rotates around the Sun. When it does this, it looks like the Sun is moving across the sky. As the Sun "moves," it makes shadows in different directions, like it did for the chopstick in the flowerpot. Watch your sundial every day. You will notice that the shadow is in pretty much the same place at the same time every day.

Beaker Bonus: The sundial was created in ancient China and Egypt thousands of years ago. The largest sundial is in Walt Disney World. It is 122 feet around at the base and 120 feet high.

Science Sleuth—Sunlight

The Sun is 93 million miles from Earth. It is a star. There are many stars that are much bigger than the Sun, but it seems big to us because it is closer than the others. And it is much bigger than the Earth. You could fit more than a million Earths inside our Sun!

The Sun is the center of our solar system. There are eight other planets that orbit around the Sun besides the Earth.

The Sun causes the weather on Earth. It helps plants make food so they can survive, and those plants provide food for other animals. The Sun also gives us light and heat.

It takes 24 hours for the Earth to turn once. This is what causes daylight and nighttime. It is day on the part of the Earth that is facing the Sun, and night on the part of the Earth that is facing away from the Sun.

Sometimes there is an eclipse of the Sun. When this happens, the Moon moves between the Earth and the Sun. The Moon blocks out the light of the Sun, so only the light around the edges shows. Even though the Moon is much smaller than the Sun, they look the same size on Earth during an eclipse because they are so far away. Total eclipses do not happen very often. The next one will be on August 11, 1999!

An eclipse

 Try this:
- Make daylight. Shine a flashlight on a globe. Notice where it is daytime and where it is night. When it is daylight in the United States, where is it night?
- Get a book on eclipses out of the library. Study up, and then try to view the next solar eclipse.

Solar Oven

Can you cook with the sun?

You'll need:

shoebox with a lid
aluminum foil
masking tape
scissors
1 Popsicle® stick
hot dogs
marshmallows

1. Line the shoebox and the lid with the aluminum foil. Be sure the shiny side is facing up. Keep the foil very smooth. Tape the foil to the edge of the box.

2. 🛑 With help, use the scissors to cut a flap in the lid of the box. It should be one inch from three sides of the lid (see below). Fold the reflecting lid back so it sticks up. Put tape around the edges of the opening to keep the foil in place.

3. Place the lid on the box. Use the Popsicle® stick and masking tape to hold the flap open.

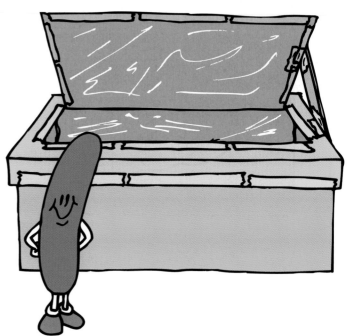

4. Place the oven in the sun. Be sure the lid is on the box and the flap is open. (You should wear sunscreen, sunglasses, and a hat for this part of the experiment.) The sun rays should be reflecting into the oven. Place a hot dog or marshmallow on a stick. Hold it in the center of the oven. It could take a while. 🛑 Be careful once it is cooked. It will be hot!

5. Line the bottom of the box with black paper. Try to cook another hot dog or marshmallow. What happens?

What happens? The first hot dog cooks in the oven. The second hot dog doesn't cook when you cover the bottom of the oven with black paper.

Why? Solar ovens use the sun's energy to create heat. The sun's rays bounce off the reflector and into the box. When they reach the box, they are reflected off the aluminum foil that is on all sides of the box. This brings all the energy together in the middle of the box. All those light molecules rubbing together make heat, which cooks your hot dog. But when you cover the foil with the black paper, the sun's rays do not reflect and bounce anymore. They are absorbed by the black paper, and the hot dog does not cook.

Sun-Baked Apples

Use your solar oven to make a delicious dessert.

You will need:
large piece of aluminum foil
slices of apple
brown sugar
raisins
cinnamon
margarine

1. Place the foil on a table. Put the apple slices and some raisins in the center of the foil.

2. Sprinkle the apples with the brown sugar and the cinnamon.

3. Place a few dots of margarine on the top of the apples.

4. Fold up the aluminum foil so the ingredients won't leak out.

5. Cook the apples in your solar oven. *Mmmmm!!!*

Kaleidoscope

How does light make this fun toy so beautiful?

You'll need:

8-inch square piece of thick black cardboard

8-inch square piece of aluminum foil

scissors

glue

tape

plastic wrap

glitter

clear or see-through balloon

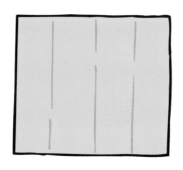

1. Fold the cardboard in half once and then again to make a long rectangle. Then unfold the cardboard to show four sections.

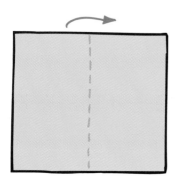

2. Place the aluminum foil, with the shiny side facing you, on the cardboard. Fold back one edge of the foil so that one section of the folded cardboard is showing. Cut off this end piece of foil along the fold.

3. Glue the larger piece of foil to the cardboard. One section of the carboard should still be showing.

4. Fold the cardboard, with the foil inside, to make a triangle-shaped tube. The section of cardboard with no foil should NOT show on the inside of the tube. Tape this cardboard section down.

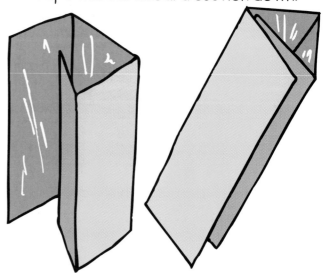

5. Cover both ends of the tube with plastic wrap. Tape the wrap to the outside of the tube. Be sure it is pulled tight.

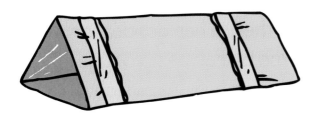

6. Pour the glitter into the clear balloon. Cut the thin mouthpiece off the balloon. Slide the opening of the balloon over one end of the cardboard tube. The balloon should be flat and tight against the end of the tube. Tape the balloon to the tube.

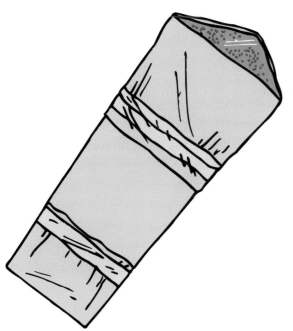

7. Hold the kaleidoscope up to a window and turn it to see the patterns it makes.

What happens? The colored glitter makes fancy patterns in the end of the kaleidoscope.

Why? Light comes through the clear balloon and reflects off the aluminum foil. The colors of the sparkles reflect off the foil. And because there are three sides to the kaleidoscope, each side reflects off the others. That is what makes the patterns that you see.

Plants

You enjoy plants and trees every day. You see them when you walk outside. Or maybe Mom grows them in her garden, or even in your house. Plants help you breathe by releasing oxygen into the air. Many animals eat plants, including humans, which means plants help you stay healthy. When you study plants, you are studying the science of botany.

Terrarium

Can you grow plants that don't need to be watered every day?

You'll need:

a 2-liter plastic soda bottle

scissors

soil

small rocks

small plants (with roots)

water

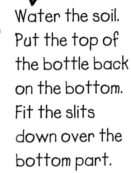

1. **STOP** Ask a grown-up to cut three inches from the bottom of the soda bottle. Then ask your helper to make six 1-inch slits around the bottom edge of the top section of the bottle as shown. Be sure the cap is on the bottle top.

2. Fill the bottom of the bottle with the rocks.

3. Dig up some soil from outside. Put it in the bottle bottom, on top of the rocks. Dig up some plants (with roots) and plant them in the soil.

4. Water the soil. Put the top of the bottle back on the bottom. Fit the slits down over the bottom part.

5. Put your terrarium in a sunny spot. It should live for a long time.

What happens? Your plants live without any extra water, food, or soil.

Why? Everything your plant needs, except light, is inside the bottle. The plant changes the sun's energy into food through *photosynthesis* (foe-toe-sin-the-sis). The plant also cleans and breathes its own air, and the soil provides the nutrients it needs. When it "exhales" it puts moisture in the air, which gives it the water it needs.

Soil Be Gone

What do plants need to grow?

You'll need:

markers
Styrofoam® cup
cotton balls
water
grass seeds
large zippered plastic bag
empty Styrofoam®
   egg carton

some planting materials: sand, crumpled
   tissues, pebbles, sawdust, cat litter,
   tea leaves, coffee grounds, rocks,
   Kellogg's® Rice Krispie's®, or shredded
   newspaper
soil
radish seeds
old shirt with a pocket
clothes hanger
large plastic bag

Experiment One:

1. Use markers to draw a face on the Styrofoam® cup.

2. Soak the cotton balls in water. Place them inside the cup.

3. Sprinkle some grass seeds over the cotton balls.

4. Put the cup in a zippered plastic bag. Zipper it closed.

5. When the grass begins to sprout, take the cup out of the bag. Your cup character looks like it's growing hair! Keep the cup in a sunny spot, and don't forget to water it once in awhile.

Experiment Two:

1. Fill one section of the empty egg carton with some soil. Fill the rest of the sections with anything you want—sand, rocks, coffee grounds, tea leaves, Kellogg's® Rice Krispie's®, etc.

2. Plant some radish seeds in each section of the carton. Water the seeds every day. Which of the plants grow?

Experiment Three:

1. Sprinkle some grass seeds in the pocket of the shirt. Hang it on a hanger. Put the large plastic bag over the shirt and knot it at the bottom. Water the pocket often.

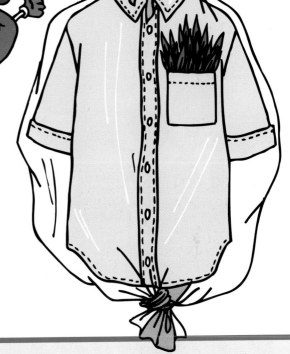

What happens? Most of your plants sprout. However they probably won't live as time goes by.

Why? Plants don't actually need soil to sprout. They need water, oxygen, sunlight, and nutrients. But soil is the best way for them to get all these things. It IS possible to get a plant to sprout without soil, but it can't live that way. Plant roots need something to attach themselves to, or a plant will fall over. They can't just grab onto water! Soil is great for roots. And it is very hard for oxygen to flow through water and reach a plant. But soil makes it easy. And water, sand, and shirt pockets don't have all the nutrients that a plant needs to continue growing.

Science Sleuth—Plants

Plants lived on earth long before there were people or animals. The first plants only lived in or near water. Now there are thousands of different plants that live on land.

Plants are important to people in many ways. We use the wood from trees to build houses and furniture. And if there were no plants, we couldn't eat. We eat many plants when we eat salads, spinach, broccoli, carrots, and all kinds of vegetables and fruits. And bread is made from grains that come from plants. When we eat eggs, hamburgers, hot dogs, or many other foods, we are eating products that come from animals. And those animals eat plants.

What do plants eat? Well, plants make their own food!

The roots of a plant drink up water from the soil. The leaves of the plant breathe in carbon dioxide from the air.

Chlorophyll is found in a plant's leaves. Chlorophyll is a green chemical. With the help of the sun, chlorophyll combines the carbon dioxide and the water taken in by the roots to make sugar. That sugar is the plant's food. When a plant makes its own food, it is called *photosynthesis* (foe-toe-sin-the-sis).

Once the plant has made sugar, it has some oxygen left over. The plant doesn't need the oxygen, so it "exhales" the oxygen into the air. You breathe in that oxygen. You exhale extra carbon dioxide that the plants use to make their food.

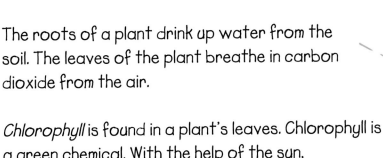

Oxygen

Carbon dioxide

 Try this:
- Start a plant parts collection. Find different kinds of fruit, nuts, bark, leaves, or seeds. How many different types can you find?
- Start a living plant collection. Start planting and growing different kinds of plants. Do certain plants need different amounts of water and sunlight than others?
- Visit a nursery or a greenhouse to discover new kinds of plants and flowers.

Growing Plants From Vegetables

When can a vegetable act like a seed?

You'll need:

potato
onion
2 glass jars with wide mouths
toothpicks
2 flowerpots
soil
water
knife

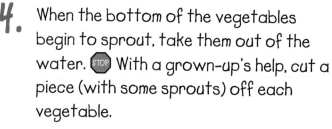

1. Fill both jars with water.

2. Stick the toothpicks into the potato and onion as shown below. Place the potato in one jar and the onion in the other. The bottom of each vegetable should sit in the water. The toothpicks should be resting on top of the jar.

3. Check the jars every day. Be sure to keep them filled with water.

4. When the bottom of the vegetables begin to sprout, take them out of the water. **STOP** With a grown-up's help, cut a piece (with some sprouts) off each vegetable.

5. Use the flowerpots and soil to plant each vegetable chunk. You should totally cover the piece of vegetable with the soil. Water the pot daily. What happens?

What happens? You grow potato and onion plants in your flowerpots.

Why? Some plants can grow without seeds. They can grow from a piece of themselves. It is called *vegetative propagation* (vej-a-tate-iv prop-a-gay-shun).

Sponge Sprouts

Can you grow plants on a kitchen sponge?

You'll need:

new sponge
bean sprouts or mustard seeds
plastic plate
plastic wrap
spray bottle
scissors
water

1. 🛑 With a grown-up's help, cut the sponge into a fancy shape—try a star or a heart or a car or a dinosaur.

2. Soak the sponge with water. Squeeze out the extra, so it does not drip.

3. Put the sponge on the plate. Sprinkle the seeds onto the sponge. Place the plate in a well-lit spot.

4. Use the spray bottle to water your sponge several times throughout each day. When you go to bed at night, cover the sponge with the plastic wrap.

5. It will take about two weeks for the seeds to sprout. Then, take a taste of your "garden."

What happens? Your seeds sprout.

Why? This is like the Soil Be Gone experiments on pages 72–73. A seed contains its own nutrients. When you provide the water and the sunlight, the plants can grow without being planted in soil. But if you want your plants to keep on living, plant them in a flowerpot or outside in the garden.

A Tree Grows

How can you sprout your own tree?

You'll need:

bowl
flowerpot
saucer
potting soil
stones
plastic bag
rubber band
acorns or orange pits
water
digging tool
compost
mulch

1. Place your acorns in the bowl. Fill the bowl with warm water. Let the acorns soak in the water overnight.

2. With a grown-up's help, peel the shells off the acorns (use your fingers—do not cut them off).

3. Put some stones in the bottom of the flowerpot. Sit the flowerpot on top of the saucer.

4. Pour the potting soil into the flowerpot until it is filled two-thirds of the way. Pour enough water on the soil to make it moist.

If you could see through the flowerpot, it would look like this.

5. Place one acorn on top of the soil. Pour more soil on top of the acorn.

6. Put a plastic bag over the top of the flowerpot. Wrap a rubber band around the bag to keep it in place. This will keep the soil moist. Put the pot in a sunny spot.

If you could see through the flowerpot, it would look like this.

7. As soon as the acorn starts to sprout through the soil, take the plastic bag off.

8. Water your seedling twice a week to keep the soil moist.

9. In the spring, plant your tree outside. To plant the tree:

- Dig a hole as deep as the pot and twice as wide as the pot.
- Mix the dirt with some compost.
- Carefully remove the plant from the pot and place it in the hole.
- Spread mulch around the base of the tree.
- Water it at least once a week during the first season.

What happens? The acorn sprouts into a seedling. The seedling grows into a tree.

Why? The acorn is a seed from a tree. If you plant it, it will grow into a new tree.

Carnation Creation

How does a flower drink when it gets thirsty?

You'll need:
measuring cup
2 glasses
white carnation with a long stem
scissors
red and blue food coloring (or any two colors)
water

1. **STOP** Ask a grown-up to cut the carnation stem lengthwise from the bottom to halfway up toward the flower.

2. Pour a 1/2 cup of water into each glass.

3. Add a different color of food coloring to each glass until the color is very dark.

4. Put one half of the flower stem in the blue water and the other half in the red water as shown.

5. Leave the carnation in the colored water for two days.

What happens? The carnation flower changes color—one half is blue, the other half is red.

Why? There are tiny tubes inside a flower stem that go from the roots up to the petals. They are called *xylem* (ZIE lem). Plants and flowers need to "drink" plenty of water in order to live. The xylem are the tubes that the water travels through to get from one part of the plant to the other. The colored water is absorbed by the bottom of your carnation's stem, and travels up to the thirsty petals. Nutrients and minerals in the soil travel through a plant the same way that the colored water travels through the flower.

Animals

What is your favorite animal? Do you have any pets at home? Some animals are a lot like people. They breathe like us. They eat like us. They take care of their children like Mom and Dad take care of you. But many animals are very different from us. They eat different things. They live in big groups. They fly south for the winter. There are millions of animals in this world, so it would take a lot of time to study them all. When you study biology, you will learn about animals and other living things.

Fruit Fly Farm

Breed your own pet fruit flies.

You'll need:

3 big glass jars
very ripe banana
grapes
paper towels
cotton (large pieces, not cotton balls)
paper
clear tape
small clear bottle
aluminum foil
magnifying glass

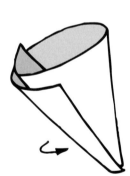

1. In one jar, put half a banana (with the peel still on) and some grapes. Crumple up one paper towel and put it in the jar also. Stuff some cotton into the top of the jar. Make sure the cotton fits tightly into the top, so the flies can't get in or out.

2. Curve a piece of paper into a funnel, as shown. (The small end of the funnel should have a 1/2-inch opening.) Tape the ends of the funnel together so it keeps its shape. Put the other half of the banana, some grapes, and a crumpled paper towel into the second jar. Place the funnel on top. This funnel will let the fruit flies into the jar, but makes it hard for them to get back out.

3. Put both jars in a warm spot. They should be in the light, but make sure the sun is not directly on the jars. Watch the jars for a few days.

4. When you see at least five fruit flies in the funnel jar, take the funnel out. Stuff cotton into the top of this jar like you did with the first jar. Keep watching the flies for about one month to see their full life cycle.

For a closer look:

With a grown-up's help, move two of the flies into the small, clear bottle. Cover $2/3$ of the bottle with aluminum foil, as shown. Fruit flies like the light, so they will move to the bottom of the bottle. Use a magnifying glass to see them up close.

Are you lucky enough to have a male and a female in your bottle? (A female fruit fly is bigger than a male. A male fruit fly has a larger, darker stripe around its body.) If you do, try putting them into the third glass jar. Add some fruit and stuff more cotton in the top. The flies should lay eggs and then you can raise even more fruit flies.

What happens? After a few days you will see larvae on the fruit. Little capsules will take their place, and eventually fruit flies will appear.

Why? Fruit flies like the smell of fruit. They find the fruit and lay eggs on it. These eggs become larvae, or maggots. After about a week, the larvae will be gone and you will see little capsules. These are the maggots in the pupae stage, which means they are resting. Finally they break out of their little cocoons as adult flies.

Scientists study fruit flies to understand *genetics* (juh-ne-tics), the study of how living things pass on traits. Humans and other animals live for a long time. But since a fruit fly lives for only a month, it is easy for a scientist to study the children, grandchildren, great-grandchildren, and so on.

Science Sleuth– Amazing Animal Facts

Decide whether the statements below are true or false. See the answers on page 151.

A. In Asia, there is a deer that is only nine inches high called the mouse deer.

B. Mayflies live for two hours.

C. The albatross can take a nap while it flies!

D. When chimpanzees say hello to each other, they touch noses.

E. When a gorilla is mad, it closes its eyes.

F. All mosquitoes bite.

G. A giraffe has the same number of neck bones as a human–seven.

H. No two zebras have the same stripes.

I. Julius Caesar had a pet giraffe.

J. Charles V of Spain had no pets.

K. King Louis IX of France had a pet elephant and a pet porcupine.

L. Napoléon and Josephine had a dog.

Fill in the blanks in the following sentences. See the answers on page 151.

1. The largest animal is the _____, at 100 feet long and 150 tons.

2. The tallest animal is the _____–it's 20 feet high.

3. The largest snake is the _____, at almost 28 feet long!

4. The largest bird is the _____, which is 9 feet tall.

5. A _____ can live for ten days without a head.

6. A _____ can fly straight up, backward, and upside down–no other bird can do that!

7. _____ must eat 250 pounds of plants and drink 50 gallons of water each day to live.

8. A hummingbird may fly to _____ different flowers every day.

9. Slugs have four _____.

10. George Washington had a pet _____ named Polly.

11. President John Quincy Adams had a pet _____.

12. Abraham Lincoln's pet was a _____ named Jack.

13. Theodore Roosevelt had a pet garter snake named _____.

14. Calvin Coolidge had a pet _____, a pet _____, and two pet _____.

15. For every person in the world, there are _____ insects.

 Try this:

• Use these fun facts to make up your own game about animals.

Ant Farm

Watch how ants work together in their colony.

You'll need:

large glass jar with
    a big opening
glass jar that will fit inside the large jar
cheesecloth
thick rubber band
damp soil from your yard
bits of leftover food
ants

1. Put about two inches
   of soil in the bottom of the large jar.

2. Use the small jar to collect some ants
   from your yard. Place the small jar
   upside down, inside the large jar. Fill the
   large jar with soil, around
   the small jar.

3. Put some food scraps on top of the soil
   in the jar. Place the cheesecloth over the
   opening in the jar. Wrap the rubber band
   around the cheesecloth to keep it in
   place.

4. Watch your ants for awhile and see
   what they create. When you are done,
   put your ants back outside.

 **What happens?** The ants
work together so they
all can live. Some collect
food. Some lay eggs.
They all have their own
job.

Why? Ants are social insects. That
means they live together (in a colony)
and help each other out.

2"

Fish Gotta Swim

How do fish move through the water?

You'll need:

large balloon
a few small rubber bands
plastic milk container
large bowl of water
paper clip
scissors
plastic knife
drinking straw

3. 🛑 With help, cut two fish-tail shapes out of the milk carton, like the one below. Place one tail on each side of the balloon's neck. Wrap a rubber band around the tails to attach them. Use a paper clip to hold the back of the two tails together.

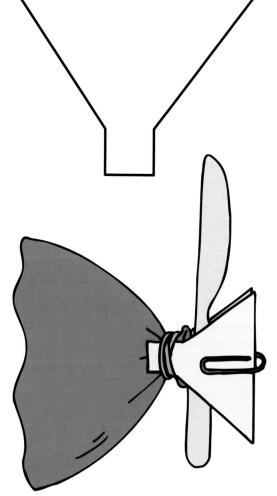

1. Fill the balloon halfway with water. Over the sink, stick the straw into the balloon opening. Hold the neck of the balloon closed so the water doesn't shoot out.

2. Wrap a rubber band around the neck of the balloon. Be sure it is tight enough so no water drips out. Bend the straw in half. Wrap another rubber band around the straw to keep it bent.

4. Slide the plastic knife between the two fish tails. (The sharp edge should face up.) Place your balloon fish into the big bowl of water.

5. Press your finger against the front of the "fish" so it does not move back and forth. Hold the plastic knife and push the fish through the water. Watch how it swims.

What happens? The fish's tail moves from side to side, and the fish moves forward.

Why? As it pushes the water aside, the fish moves forward.

Beaker Bonus: There is a fish called the cosmopolitan sailfish that was tested for its speed. It was clocked at about 68 miles per hour, which is faster than a cheetah.

Worm Farm

What kind of home does an earthworm like?

You'll need:
quart-size jar
2 cups of soil
1 cup of decaying leaves and roots (humus)
earthworms (you can dig up your own or
    buy them at a bait-and-tackle shop)
peelings from an apple
dark construction paper
rubber band
water

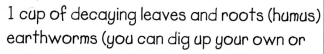

1. Put the soil in the jar. Pour a little water onto the soil. Sprinkle the humus over the soil.

2. Place the worms in the jar. Put the apple peelings inside, too. Place a dark piece of con-struction paper over the top of the jar, as shown. Wrap a rubber band around it.

3. Put the jar in a cool area. Take the paper off the jar every day for a week to watch your earthworms.

What happens? The earthworms disappear under the soil. So do the apple peels! You can see little tunnels in the soil.

Why? Earthworms live in the soil. They EAT soil. A muscle inside their bodies sucks in the dirt. They take food out of the soil, and then the soil passes through their bodies.

Earthworms absorb oxygen from the soil through their moist skin. Earthworms are good for soil. They make it richer in certain nutrients. You can find about 50,000 worms in one acre of soil.

Beaker Bonus: Around 1937, in South Africa, a giant earthworm was found that was 22 feet long and almost an inch around!

Science Sleuth—Animal Names

Match the name for an animal baby with its adult name. See the answers on page 151.

a. cub	1. giraffe
b. nymph	2. fox
c. fawn	3. seal
d. foal	4. kangaroo
e. calf	5. bear
f. fry	6. deer
g. cub	7. goose
h. nestling	8. cockroach
i. gosling	9. donkey
j. calf	10. fish
k. joey	11. nightingale
l. bunny	12. elephant
m. whelp	13. rabbit
n. calf	14. swan
o. poult	15. whale
p. cygnet	16. turkey

Match the single animal with its proper group of animals. See the answers on page 151.

a. ant	1. kennel
b. bear	2. band
c. cat	3. clutch
d. cow	4. pace
e. chick	5. colony
f. dog	6. sloth
g. donkey	7. clutter
h. duck	8. drove
i. fox	9. brood
j. gorilla	10. leash
k. hare	11. pride
l. hen	12. brace
m. kangaroo	13. down
n. leopard	14. block
o. lion	15. nest
p. nightingale	16. leap
q. pig	17. pod
r. rabbit	18. bevy
s. seal	19. watch
t. sheep	20. troop
u. swan	21. litter
v. whale	22. trip

Try this:
- Visit the zoo. How many different animals can you find?

Outdoor Science

There are a lot of things to learn about in nature. Besides plants and animals, there are earthquakes, hurricanes, tornados, volcanos, and the weather. Nature affects what we eat, what you find in the grocery store, when it is sunny, and when it snows. When you study the weather, you are studying meteorology.

Making Lightning

What causes lightning?

You'll need:
2 balloons
a wool mitten

1. With a grown-up's help, blow up both balloons.

2. Rub one balloon on the mitten. Rub the other balloon against a wall.

3. Make the room dark. Slowly move the two balloons toward each other. What happens?

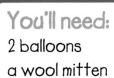

What happens? You see light sparks as the balloons get closer together.

Why? The balloons, the wall, and the mitten have negative and positive electrical charges in them. Everything does. When you rub these objects together, you change the charges. One balloon becomes more negatively charged, and the other becomes more positive. Opposite charges are attracted to each other. When you move the balloons together, the one that is more positive is attracted to the one that is more negative. The tiny negatively charged particles begin to jump toward the positive balloon. This creates *static electricity.*

Lightning is like this. The clouds and the ground have opposite charges so the negative particles in the cloud begin to jump toward the positive particles of the ground. This creates static electricity, which is why we see lightning.

Right this minute, there are about 1,800 *thunderstorms* happening in the world. Every second, 100 bolts of lightning strike the earth.

Lightning can be very dangerous. It can cause fires. It can hurt people and animals. It can damage houses and buildings. But we need lightning. It evens out the amount of *electricity* in the sky and on the ground.

Lightning is caused by *electrons*. Electrons are tiny little particles that make up *atoms*. Everything—people, animals, plants, air, water—is made up of atoms.

Electrons are full of electrical energy. When there is a storm, the clouds in the sky release drops of water. While all this water is moving around, atoms are bumping into each other. When atoms bump into each other, electrons are sometimes swapped between them.

Electrons are negatively charged. Atoms that lose electrons have a positive charge. Atoms that gain new electrons have a negative charge. Loose electrons are also negative, and are attracted to atoms that have a positive charge. These loose electrons will shoot toward the positive atoms. When this happens they are moving so fast that they make the air around them glow. That's when you see lightning.

Lightning strikes are usually about three miles long, but only about an inch wide! Lightning causes thunder. When lightning strikes, it makes the air around it hot. When air gets hot, its molecules get bigger. As they quickly expand and bump into each other, they give off vibrations. These vibrations sound like thunder to you.

 Try this:

- Borrow a book about Benjamin Franklin from the library. How did he learn about lightning? What did he learn?
- Bite into a wintergreen Lifesaver® in the dark. It should make a spark. Why do you think this happened?
- Try to figure out how far away the lightning is during the next storm. For every five seconds you can count between lightning and thunder, the lightning strike is one mile away.

Finger Time

Can you tell what time it is just by looking at the sun?

You'll need:
your fingers
a sunny day

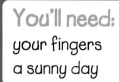

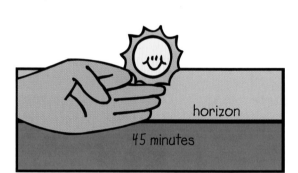

30 minutes

1. Stand outside, facing the sun, so you can see a horizon line.

45 minutes

2. Stretch your arm out in front of you. Line your pinky finger up with the horizon line, and stack your other fingers on top until they reach the sun. (See below.)

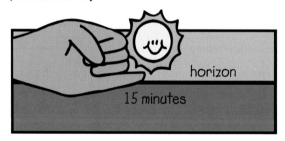

15 minutes

60 minutes or 1 hour

3. To tell the time, count how many fingers you have stacked up. Every four fingers is one hour. So if you have four fingers stacked up, and it's the morning, you know it has been one hour since sunrise. In the afternoon, it would be about one hour until the sun sets.

What happens? You can tell how many hours since sunrise or until sunset by how high the sun is above the horizon line.

The Tornado Machine

What makes a tornado?

You'll need:

2 two-liter soda pop bottles
3 inches of rigid tubing with the same size
   opening as the bottle (5/8)
water

1. Fill one bottle to the top of the neck with water. Put a 3/4-inch length of the tubing into the bottle's opening.

2. Hold the mouth of the empty bottle over the mouth of the bottle filled with water. Insert a 3/4-inch length of the remaining tubing into the empty bottle as shown.

3. With a grown-up's help, turn the water-filled bottle upside down so it is on top of the empty bottle. Water from the top bottle will begin to fall into the empty one. Spin the water-filled bottle counterclockwise while you shake it. (If this is hard, ask your grown-up helper to give it a try.)

What happens? The water starts to whirl, forming a funnel-shaped air column in the center.

Why? Because the water on top is heavier, it falls down into the empty bottle. There is not enough room for all the air in the bottom bottle when this happens, so some air moves upward into the water-filled bottle. When you spin and shake the top bottle, the water falls in a circular motion. It makes a little passage in the middle, through which the air passes.

In a real tornado, a mass of cold, heavy, dry air meets up with warm, moist air. Because the cold air is heavier, it usually moves under the warmer air. But sometimes the cold air moves over the warm air. Scientists don't understand why this happens. Then the lighter warm air moves up through the cold air with the help of strong winds. There is low pressure in the middle of the cold air, and a funnel-shaped tornado is formed.

How Molecules Act

Have you ever watched atoms and molecules move and change? Sure you have! When things melt, or when they freeze, you are watching atoms and molecules. When you cook, turn on a light, or blow a bubble, you are watching particles at work. Everything is made up of atoms and molecules.

Sherbet

What does a freezer do to molecules?

You'll need:
2 large lemons
2 cups sugar
4 cups milk
grater

1. With help, squeeze the juice from both lemons into a bowl.

2. **STOP** Ask a grown-up to help you grate the rind from one of the lemons. Mix the rind with the lemon juice.

3. Add the sugar to the lemon juice. Slowly stir in the milk.

4. Pour the mixture into a small pan. Put the pan in the freezer.

5. When the mixture is partially frozen, take it out of the freezer. Stir it to break up any large ice crystals that may have formed.

6. Put the mixture back in the freezer. Let it freeze completely, and then dig in!

What happens? You turn a liquid into a solid.

Why? The sherbet mixture is warmer than anything else in the freezer. The heat molecules flow from the sherbet mixture to the colder air around it in the freezer. As the heat leaves the sherbet, it gets colder and starts to freeze. The molecules in the mixture start moving more slowly and bond together to make crystals. These crystals make a solid called sherbet that you can eat.

Hot-Air Mobiles

Can heat make things move?

You'll need:
construction paper
scissors
four 12-inch pieces of
    thread
4 paper clips
hanger
lamp

1. (STOP) With help cut a 4-inch circle from the construction paper. Fold the circle in half. Fold it in half again. Fold it in half a third time.

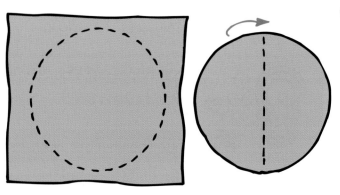

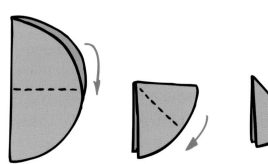

2. Unfold the circle. Make a dot on each fold, 1/2 inch from the edge of the circle as shown. (STOP) Cut on each fold, up to the dot. Fold back one side of every slit.

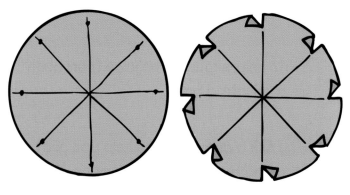

3. Tie a piece of thread to one paper clip. Poke a hole in the middle of the circle. Pull the free end of the thread through the hole. When the thread is in the right place, the paper clip hangs down in the middle and the folded corners face down.

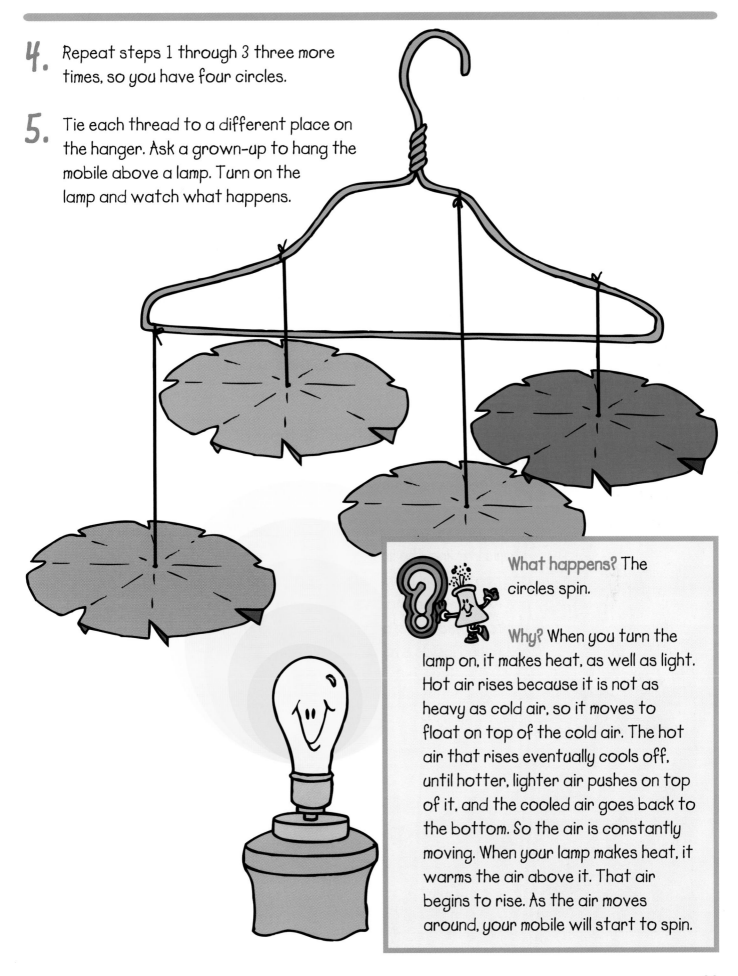

4. Repeat steps 1 through 3 three more times, so you have four circles.

5. Tie each thread to a different place on the hanger. Ask a grown-up to hang the mobile above a lamp. Turn on the lamp and watch what happens.

What happens? The circles spin.

Why? When you turn the lamp on, it makes heat, as well as light. Hot air rises because it is not as heavy as cold air, so it moves to float on top of the cold air. The hot air that rises eventually cools off, until hotter, lighter air pushes on top of it, and the cooled air goes back to the bottom. So the air is constantly moving. When your lamp makes heat, it warms the air above it. That air begins to rise. As the air moves around, your mobile will start to spin.

Science Sleuth–Atoms

Everything is made up of *atoms*. You are. So is your dog. And your house and car. And rocks, plants, water, the sky, and everything else.

There are a little more than 100 types of atoms. Different kinds of atoms can join together to make new substances.

Atoms are very small. If you placed ten million atoms in a line, the line would measure only one centimeter! But there are particles that are even smaller than atoms! There are *protons, neutrons,* and *electrons* and they are found inside atoms.

An atom

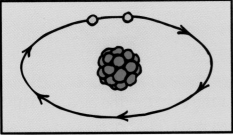

The *nucleus* of an atom is formed by all the protons and neutrons joining together in the center of the atom. The electrons move around the nucleus. The path the electron follows is an *energy level.*

Atoms make up *elements.* An element is a simple substance. You can't divide it up into other substances. But you can add it to another element. When two elements have a chemical reaction, they form *molecules* and make a new substance or *compound.*

Elements are things like oxygen, hydrogen, nitrogen, and helium. The atoms that make up different elements each have a different number of protons, neutrons, and electrons. This is what makes one kind of atom different from another.

 Try this:
- Make a model of an atom. Find things around the house to use as the nucleus, energy levels, electrons, protons, and neutrons.

Rock Candy

Watch crystals form when you make a delicious candy.

You'll need:
4 Popsicle® sticks
4 small glasses
2 cups sugar
4 1/2 cups water
food coloring

1. Put the sugar and water in a saucepan. Stir it with a wooden spoon. The sugar may not dissolve in the water right away.

2. (STOP) Ask a grown-up to heat the mixture on the stove top until it starts to boil. Stir it once in awhile. Let it boil for two minutes.

3. Make sure the four glasses feel warm. If they don't, run them under some hot water.

4. Divide the sugar and water solution equally among the four glasses. Add a little food coloring to each glass (you can use a different color in each). Put one Popsicle® stick in each glass and stir.

5. Leave the sticks in the glasses. Put the glasses in a well-lit area. Leave them for a week. Check on the glasses at least once a day to see what is happening.

6. At the end of the week, taste your creation!

What happens? Crystals form around the wooden sticks, making rock-candy lollipops.

Why? When you put the sugar in the water, you make a *supersaturated* solution. This means that there is so much of a solid in a liquid, the solid can't dissolve anymore. When you leave the solution out in the glasses, the water starts to evaporate. As the water disappears, it leaves just the sugar, which reforms into crystals that attach to the wooden stick.

A Balloon Trick

How do you keep a balloon from popping?

3. With help, push the jellied end of the stick through the bottom of the balloon, next to where the knot is tied and where it is darker in color. Push it all the way through the balloon until it comes out the top.

You'll need:

a few 8-inch by 10-inch round balloons
thin wooden shish-kebab skewer
petroleum jelly

1. Ask a grown-up to blow up one of the balloons (about halfway). Tie the end of the balloon in a knot. Stick the shish-kebab stick into the side of the balloon. What happens?

What happens? The first balloon pops and the second does not.

Why? Balloons are made from rubber. Rubber is a material that has many molecules linked together. These molecules try very hard to stay together. The first balloon pops because the skewer is pushed through where the rubber is most stretched. The second time you push the stick through, you put it through a part of the balloon where the rubber is not very stretched (notice that these areas are darker than the middle of the balloon). So the molecules pull apart just a little, letting the stick through.

2. Ask a grown-up to blow up another balloon. Rub petroleum jelly on the end of the stick.

PETROLEUM JELLY

Science Sleuth—Energy

When something happens, there is energy. When you walk, there is energy. When you sweat, there is energy. When you watch TV, there is energy. But it is not all the same kind of energy.

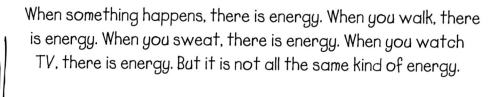

Heat Energy—Heat makes molecules move faster. Heat moves energy from place to place, because heat will move from hot substances to cold substances. When you put ice cubes in a glass of juice, the ice is colder than the juice. The heat energy from the juice transfers to the ice until they are both the same temperature.

Light Energy—When an object gets very hot, it will glow. This makes light. The sun, lightbulbs, and campfires are all examples of light energy.

Sound Energy—Sounds are created by movement. When something moves, it causes vibrations in the air, and our brains translate those vibrations into sound.

Electrical Energy—Electrical wires let us transfer energy from one place to another. And electrical energy can be converted into other kinds of energy, like light, heat, and sound.

Chemical Energy—When there is a chemical reaction, there is chemical energy. When substances are burned, for example, the gases that are released are a form of chemical energy.

Nuclear Energy—When scientists make changes to the nucleus of an atom, energy is often released.

 Try this:
- Look for different kinds of energy in your house. Where can you find light, heat, sound, and electrical energy?
- Find out about nuclear energy. Borrow a book from your library, and find out how it is used.
- Run in place for one minute. What kind of energy are you using?

Crystal Rock Garden

Watch crystals form in a few days.

You'll need:
glass pie plate (not metal)
different-size rocks
2 tablespoons salt
1/4 cup warm water

1. In a small bowl, mix the salt and water. Stir until the salt dissolves in the water.

2. Place your rocks in the pie plate. Pour the salt and water mixture over the rocks.

3. Put the plate in a warm, sunny spot. Let the plate sit for at least several days. Check it at least once a day. What happens?

What happens? Salt crystals grow on the rocks.

Why? Salt comes in a crystal form. When you dissolve the salt in water, you make a solution. But when you put the pie plate in the sun, the water in the solution begins to evaporate. As it does, the salt crystals are left. They begin to clump together on top of the rocks.

Find the Penny

*Can you find the right penny
in the bunch?*

You'll need:
5 pennies, each with a different year
plate
hat

1. Put the five pennies on the plate.

2. Ask a volunteer from the audience to pick one of the pennies while you hide your eyes. Tell the volunteer to look at the date, and to pass the penny around to the rest of the audience so they can see the date also.

3. Ask your volunteer to put the penny back in the hat. Tell her to pour the rest of the pennies from the plate into the hat.

4. Reach into the hat. Feel around for the penny that is warm. Pull it out and ask the volunteer if that is her penny.

What happens? You choose the penny that your volunteer picked.

Why? Pennies are made out of copper. Copper is a metal. Metals *conduct* heat easily. When your audience touches the penny, the heat from their hands is transferred to the penny, making it warmer than the ones that were on the plate.

Slick Trick

*Make a wire move mysteriously
through a block of ice.*

You'll need:

shallow plastic container
water
colored paper
glue
scissors
2 glass jars with lids
2 plastic soda bottles
thin wire
marbles or pennies

To prepare:

1. The day before your magic show, fill the plastic container halfway with water. Put the container in the freezer.

2. Use the colored paper and glue to decorate the glass jars.

3. **STOP** Ask a grown-up to cut the bottoms off the soda bottles. Then have your helper punch two equally spaced holes on one bottle bottom. Take a small length of wire and tie each end through one of the holes to make a small pail handle as shown. Repeat this with the other bottom.

4. **STOP** Ask your helper to cut off another piece of wire. Tie each end around one of the pail handles.

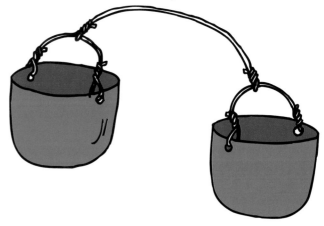

5. **STOP** Right before you do the trick, ask your helper to push the ice block out of the container.

To do the trick:

1. Ask your assistant to bring in the ice. Place it on top of the two lidded jars.

2. Place the wire that attaches the two pails over the middle of the ice block, so one pail hangs down on each side. Fill the pails with marbles or pennies so they are heavy.

3. While you are waiting, do another trick.

What happens? The wire slowly moves through the block of ice, but the ice stays in one piece.

Why? The pails are heavy and pull downward on the wire. This creates pressure on the ice, which makes heat. The heat melts the ice that is right under the wire, and the wire starts to cut through the ice.

But heat likes to move from warmer areas to cooler areas. So as the wire sinks, the molecules in the melted water on top of it start to lose their heat. The water freezes again.

Blowing Bubbles

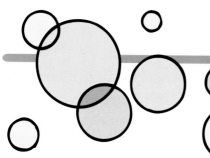

Why are bubbles round?

You'll need:

small bottle of glycerine (ask a grown-up to pick some up at the drugstore)
eyedropper
small, same-size containers
dishwashing liquid
small bubble blower from a jar of store-bought bubbles

1. Pour some dishwashing liquid into each container.

2. With the eyedropper, add a different number of glycerine drops to each container. Keep track of how many drops you put in each one.

3. Use the bubble blower to test each formula. Stick the blower in a container. Lift it out of the container. Blow. Do this with all the formulas. Which one makes the best bubbles? When you figure it out, make more of that formula.

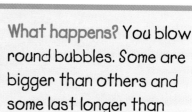

What happens? You blow round bubbles. Some are bigger than others and some last longer than others, depending on the formula.

Why? Why are bubbles round? Objects get their shapes from the *forces* that are around them. The molecules in the soap film that form a bubble are trying to stay very close together. They are pulling toward one another. The air inside the bubble is pushing outward on the soap molecules. The pushing and pulling is even all over the bubble. When this happens, an object will be round.

Making a Bubble Blower

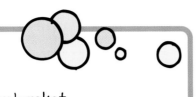

You'll need:

clothespin

plastic strawberry basket

scissors

pan

bubble mixture

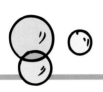

1. STOP With help, cut the bott[...] [t]he berry basket.

2. Clip the clothespin to the edge of the cut-out basket bottom.

3. Pour your soap bubble mixture into a pan. Dip the basket mesh into the mixture.

4. Blow on it or wave it in the air.

Tabletop Fun

Why don't you try making bubble creations on a table rather than in the air?

1. Find a table that a grown-up will let you play on. Pour your bubble mixture into a bowl.

2. Wet the tabletop. Wet the outside of a straw. Dip the straw into the mixture. Cover the end with your finger until it is over the table. Take your finger off the end of the straw and release the bubble mixture onto the table.

3. Blow into the straw and make one bubble or bubble twins or a line of bubbles on the table.

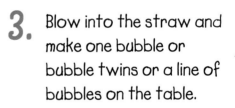

4. Or try making a bubble chain. Stand away from the table. Point the straw at your feet. Slowly blow a small bubble. Wiggle the straw back and forth to close it. Now blow a second bubble and do the same thing. See how many bubbles you can blow before the chain breaks.

The Ice-Cream Maker

Make your own ice cream without any fancy, expensive machines.

You'll need:

1 egg
2/3 cup sugar
1 teaspoon vanilla
1 cup heavy cream
2 cups half-and-half
3/4 cup cookies, crushed
empty coffee can with a plastic lid
scissors

wooden spoon
5-pound bag of ice
brown grocery bag
hammer
newspapers
bucket
2 1/2 cups of table salt
ice-cube tray

1. **STOP** Ask a grown-up to poke a small hole in the coffee-can lid. Place the hole a little to the right of the center. Stick the wooden-spoon handle through the hole. Ask your helper to trim off any excess plastic around the hole.

2. **STOP** With help, use an electric mixer to mix the egg, sugar, and vanilla for one minute on medium. Add the cream and the half-and-half. Mix on low for three minutes. Put this bowl in the refrigerator.

3. Put the bag of ice in the brown paper bag and cover it with newspapers. **STOP** Ask a grown-up to use a hammer to crush the ice.

4. Put about one-third of the ice in the bucket. Pour 1/2 cup of salt over the ice (make sure it covers the ice). Put the coffee can on top of the ice. Layer more ice and salt in the bucket around the coffee can until all the ice is gone.

If you could see through the bucket, it would look like this.

5. Pour two-thirds of the ice-cream mixture into the coffee can. Pour what is left of the ice-cream mixture into the ice-cube tray and put it in the freezer.

6. Put the lid on the coffee can, so the spoon handle sticks up.

7. Holding the wooden spoon, rotate the can continuously. Every couple of minutes, stop turning. Hold the can still and use the spoon handle to stir the ice cream inside the can. Try to touch the bottom and sides of the can as you do this.

8. After ten minutes, take the lid off the can. Pour in the crushed cookies. Put the lid back on. Keep on spinning and stirring. Once in awhile you can take the lid off to check your ice cream, but don't do this too much. It will take about a half hour total to make the ice cream.

9. As soon as the ice cream is thick, check the ice-cube tray. Which one froze faster?

What happens? Both methods made ice cream, but the coffee-can ice cream froze quicker.

Why? The salt causes the ice to melt. As the ice melts, it mixes with the salt to make saltwater. The salt lowers the temperature of the water so it is below the freezing point, but it won't freeze. The saltwater becomes colder than your freezer, so the ice cream in the can freezes more quickly than the ice cream in the freezer.

The Secret Ball

Can you find the hidden ball?

You'll need:

3 jars with lids that are exactly the same

ball that fits into the jars and is heavy enough to sink in water

oil-based paints

paintbrush

water

To prepare:

1. Paint the jars with the paint so you can't see through them.

2. Fill each jar halfway with water. Be sure each jar has exactly the same amount of water as the others.

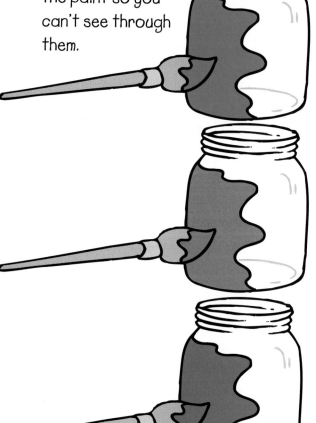

To do the trick:

1. Line up the jars next to each other on the table. Take the lids off.

2. Ask a volunteer from the audience to put the ball in one of the jars, and put the lids on all the jars while you turn away.

3. Tell your audience you know which jar has the ball inside. Tap each jar once with your wand. When you do this, the jars will make a ringing sound. Talk to your audience so they do not hear the ringing. The jar that makes the strange sound has the ball inside. When you know which it is, pick it up, unscrew the lid, and show the audience the ball inside.

What happens? The jar with the ball inside sounds different from the others.

Why? The sound a jar makes when you tap it depends on how big the jar is and how much water is in it. Before the ball goes into a jar, all three of your jars are exactly the same. Once the ball goes in, it takes up space in the jar and displaces the water. This makes the water move up higher in the jar, so when you tap it, the sound is different from the other jars.

Forces

Forces help you stand. They help you move. They help you stay in your seat. They give you strength. Forces keep everything from flying around in the air. When you study forces, you are also studying physics.

It's a "Wand-erful" Trick!

*Make a wand
that seems to float in the air.*

You'll need:

12-inch-long cardboard tube
clay
scrap paper
colored paper

paint
paintbrush
2 small same-size cardboard boxes
glue

To prepare:

1. Fill one end of the tube with the clay. Stuff scrap paper in the ends of the wand, so your audience can't see the clay. Use colored paper or paints to decorate the tube so it looks like a magic wand (white on the ends and black in the middle).

2. Decorate the boxes with the paints so they look magical.

To do the trick:

1. Put the two small boxes on the table. Lay the tube on top, so that each end is resting on one of the boxes.

2. Slowly slide the box out from under the empty end of the tube.

What happens? The tube stays where it is. It does not fall over.

Why? When you put the clay into the end of the wand, you add weight to that end. The center of gravity shifts to that end of the wand, so when you pull out the box, the center of gravity is still supported, and the wand stays balanced.

Magic Mystery Marble

Why doesn't a bead of oil dissolve in this mixture?

You'll need:
rubbing alcohol
cooking oil
blue or green food coloring
water
eyedropper
half-pint bottle

1. Pour some water in the bottle until it is half full. Add a few drops of food coloring.

2. Pour in a few teaspoonfuls of oil. Now pour in a little alcohol. What happens to the oil?

3. Keep pouring in the alcohol until the oil becomes perfectly round.

What happens? The oil becomes a perfectly round marble shape when you pour in the alcohol.

Why? When just the oil and water are in the bottle, the water stays at the bottom because it is heavier than the oil. The water pushes on the oil from below and the air pushes on the oil from above. This makes the oil become a flat layer.

When you add the alcohol, it mixes with the water and makes the water mixture lighter. Since the oil is so heavy, it begins to sink. The alcohol and water push on the oil from all directions, making it form a ball shape.

Stuck on You

What do you have to do to get up from a chair?

You'll need:
straight-backed chair

1. Sit in the chair. Keep your back flat against the back of the chair.

2. Fold your arms in front of you.

3. Stand up without leaning forword.

What happens? You cannot get out of your seat.

Why? When you sit with your arms folded, you put your center of gravity over the seat of the chair. You cannot stand unless you lean forward and shift the center of gravity over your feet.

Geronimo!

How do parachutes work?

You'll need:

5-inch square of cardboard
scissors
pipe cleaner
glue
4 tablespoons of flour
6 tablespoons of water
newspapers cut into 1/2-inch-wide strips

tempera or hobby paints
paintbrush
garbage bag
marker
needle
six 12-inch lengths of heavy thread

1. On the cardboard draw a little man that is about the size and shape of the one shown on the next page. Cut out the man.

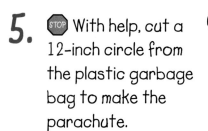

2. Twist the pipe cleaner to look like the picture below. Glue the pipe cleaner to the back of your man so the ends of the pipe cleaner are glued to his arms. Be sure the loop is not glued to your man (you will later tie the parachute to this loop).

3. Mix the flour and water together. Dip the newspaper strips into the mixture. Cover the parachute man with the strips until he gets bulky. Be sure to leave the loop uncovered. Let him dry overnight.

4. The next day, decorate your man with paint. Let him dry.

5. **STOP** With help, cut a 12-inch circle from the plastic garbage bag to make the parachute.

6. With the marker, put six dots on the circle as shown below. They should be about a 1/4 inch from the edge of the parachute.

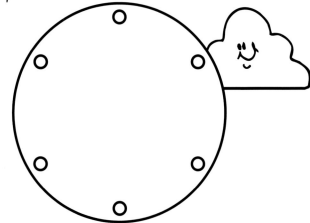

7. 🛑 With help, thread the needle with a length of thread. Poke the needle through one hole. Pull the thread through the hole so there are six inches of thread on each end of the circle. Use a 12-inch piece of string for each hole.

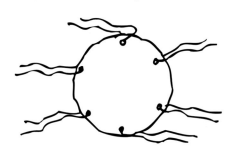

8. Gather together all the strings. (Each string is now a double strand.) Be sure they are all the same length. Tie the strings to the loop in back of your parachute man.

9. Try throwing your man up in the air. 🛑 Ask a grown-up to drop him from the top of a ladder and from other heights. What happens?

10. Try different-sized parachutes on your man. Make some smaller and some larger. (The thread for each hole should be the same size as the parachute is across.)

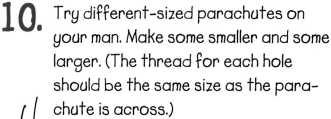

What happens? When you throw your parachute man into the air, the parachute fills up with air and decreases the speed at which he falls.

Why? Parachutes work because of gravity. Gravity is the force that holds us down to the ground. Gravity is the force that draws any two objects to each other. When someone makes a parachute jump, the force of gravity is pulling them down to the ground. The closer the jumper gets to the ground, the greater the force. The force pulls him down faster and faster. The parachute creates a resistance, and slows down the jumper. The slower the jumper, the less is the force.

Science Sleuth—
Sir Isaac Newton

Sir Isaac Newton was a mathematician in England. When he was a little boy, he did not do very well in school. But he liked to spend time doing experiments and thinking about how things worked. He explained to the world how and why things moved. These ideas are called Newton's Laws of Motion.

The first law—When something moves, it will not stop or turn or go faster or go slower until something gets in its way. It will just keep moving in a straight line.

The second law—An object will go faster depending on how strong the force is that is acting on it. For example, if you tap your sister on the back while she is sitting on a swing, she won't move very much. But if you run up from behind and push her hard with both hands, she will swing higher and faster. You are the force, and the harder you push, the higher and faster she will go.

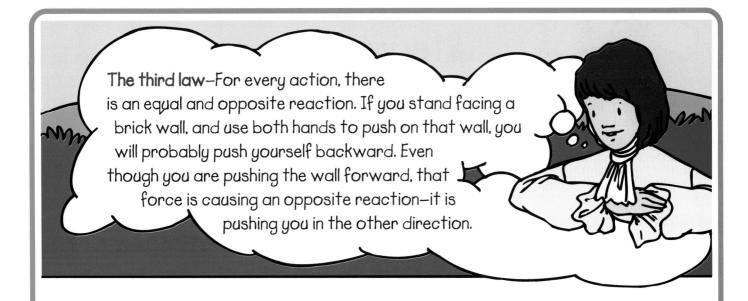

The third law—For every action, there is an equal and opposite reaction. If you stand facing a brick wall, and use both hands to push on that wall, you will probably push yourself backward. Even though you are pushing the wall forward, that force is causing an opposite reaction—it is pushing you in the other direction.

You probably agree with the second and third laws, but wonder about the first. You know that if you bounce a ball, it will eventually stop, even if you don't touch it. But forces stop the ball. There are forces that you cannot see that act on EVERYTHING.

Friction is a force that slows everything down. When two things rub together, there is friction. When you walk, your shoe rubs against the floor and makes friction. If there were no friction, things would just slide around all the time. In space, there is no friction.

The other invisible force is *gravity*. Gravity is the pull between two objects. The earth's pull on us is very strong, because it is so big. That's why we don't float around in the air. Isaac Newton "discovered" gravity when he was sitting in his orchard and an apple fell from a tree.

 Try this:
- Find examples of friction in your house. Walk around and try to find objects that are rubbing against each other. How many can you find?
- Test the first law. Roll a ball on the ground. If it doesn't keep rolling forever, what's stopping it?
- Test the second law. Tap a ball with the toe of your foot. Then push it a little harder. Then give it a good swift kick. What happens each time? Is Newton's second law correct?
- Test the third law. Push and roll different objects. What happens to your body when you do this? Do you see any equal and opposite reactions?

Steamboat

Does heat make things move?

You'll need:

pineapple
nail
empty, round peanut can with a plastic lid
water
wooden skewers
small candle in a metal holder
matches
knife

1. 🛑 Ask a grown-up to cut the pineapple in half from top to bottom. Then have him cut off the leaves.

2. Next ask your helper to scoop out the inside of the pineapple from one half. Let this empty half dry in a warm spot overnight. This is the boat.

3. 🛑 Ask your helper to use the nail to poke a small hole in the middle of the plastic lid.

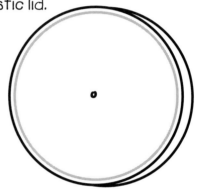

4. Pour water into the can until it is one-fourth full. Put the lid on the can.

If you could see through the can, it would look like this.

124

5. Stick the skewers through the pineapple skin, as shown below. You should be able to sit the can on top of them, and fit the candle under the can.

6. Sit the candle in the boat, underneath the skewers. (STOP) Ask a grown-up to light the candle. Then tell your helper to sit the can on its side over the candle, and then place the whole boat in a bathtub with water in it. What Happens?

What happens? The steamboat moves around the tub.

Why? The heat from the candle makes the water in the can boil. This makes steam. As more and more steam fills the can, it must find a way out. It escapes through the hole in the lid. As it does, it creates a force that pushes the boat forward.

Tumble Tower

This magical tower will stand even when you tamper with its "foundation."

You'll need:

small cardboard boxes
clay
small plastic garbage bag
tape
paint
paintbrush

To prepare:

1. Press some modeling clay into the bottom of each of the boxes to make them heavier.

2. Tape the boxes shut. Use the paints to decorate the outside of the boxes.

To do the trick:

1. Lay the plastic bag on top of a table. Place the boxes on top of the plastic, building a tower.

2. Tell the audience you will remove the plastic bag without moving the tower.

3. Hold the corners of the plastic bag. With one hard tug, pull the plastic bag straight out along the table. (This trick takes a lot of practice!)

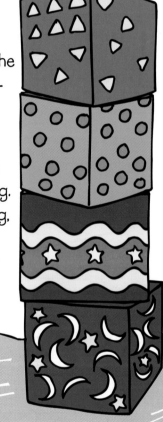

What happens? You pull the bag out, and the tower does not fall.

Why? *Gravity* is working on the tower. It pulls down on the boxes, so they stay where they are. This is called *inertia*. When you pull the plastic bag, you do it so quickly you do not create a lot of *friction*. This also keeps the boxes in place.

Chemical Changes & Reactions

You come in contact with chemical reactions every day. Many of your toys are made by chemical changes. Soap and toothpaste are made from chemical changes. Even the bread on your sandwich at lunch was made with a chemical change. When you study chemical reactions, you are studying chemistry.

Science Sleuth— Chemical Reactions

When water freezes, that is not a chemical reaction. We call it a physical change. In a physical change, the way something looks may change, but it is still made up of the same kinds of atoms. If you melt ice, you will get water again.

A chemical change makes a totally new substance. When you change a substance chemically, you can't turn it back to the way it was before.

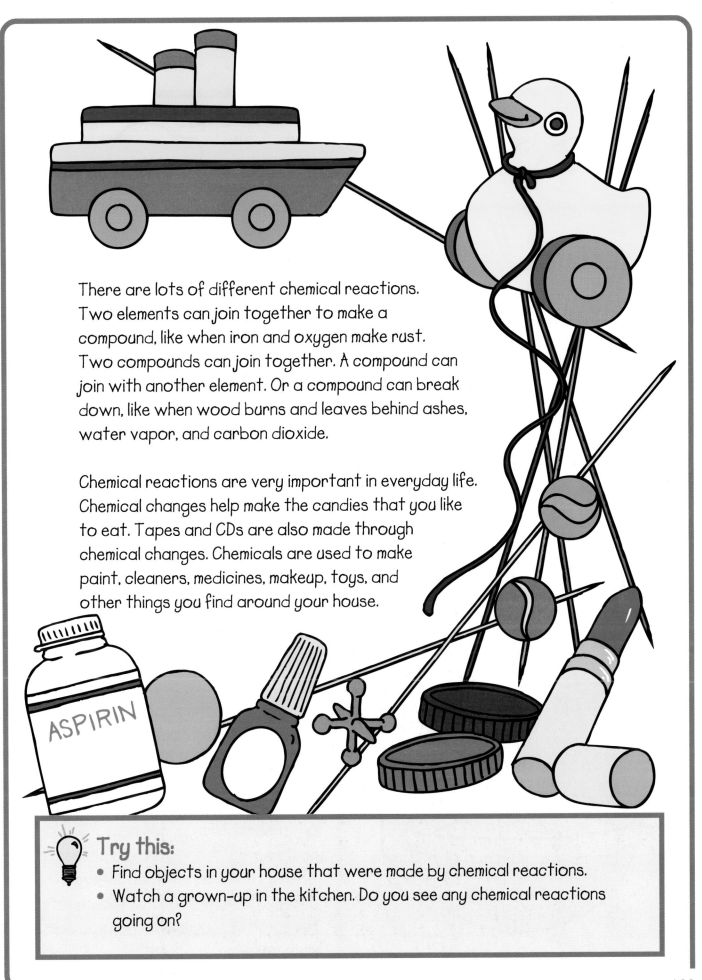

There are lots of different chemical reactions. Two elements can join together to make a compound, like when iron and oxygen make rust. Two compounds can join together. A compound can join with another element. Or a compound can break down, like when wood burns and leaves behind ashes, water vapor, and carbon dioxide.

Chemical reactions are very important in everyday life. Chemical changes help make the candies that you like to eat. Tapes and CDs are also made through chemical changes. Chemicals are used to make paint, cleaners, medicines, makeup, toys, and other things you find around your house.

ASPIRIN

Try this:
- Find objects in your house that were made by chemical reactions.
- Watch a grown-up in the kitchen. Do you see any chemical reactions going on?

Invisible Ink

How can you write and read secret messages?

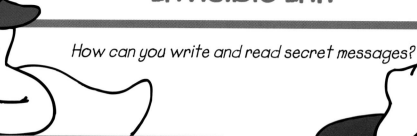

You'll need:

bottled lemon juice
paintbrush
notebook paper

1. Pour some of the lemon juice into a small bowl.

2. Dip the paintbrush in the lemon juice. Write a message on a piece of notebook paper. Let the message dry completely. Your message will be invisible.

3. Hold your paper up to a lightbulb. Move it back and forth until the paper starts to get warm. What do you see?

 **What happens?** After a few minutes of holding the paper in front of the lightbulb, your message appears.

Why? When you turn on the light, you create light energy. You also create heat energy. Lemon juice is a chemical. When it combines with heat energy, a chemical change happens. This changes the color of the juice, letting you see your message.

Presto Change-O

How do you make green pennies?

You'll need:
saucer
paper towel
vinegar
5 pennies

3. Put the pennies on top of the paper towel.

1. Tear off one paper towel. Fold it in half once. Fold it in half again to make a square.

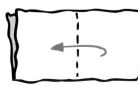

2. Put the towel on the saucer. Pour vinegar into the saucer so the towel is completely wet.

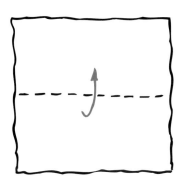

What happens? The tops of the pennies turn green.

Why? Vinegar is an acid, which is a chemical. Part of the acid combines with the copper in a penny to make a chemical reaction. When they react, they make a new substance called copper acetate, which is the green coating on the pennies.

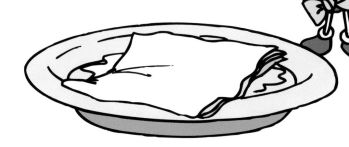

131

Make Your Own Volcano

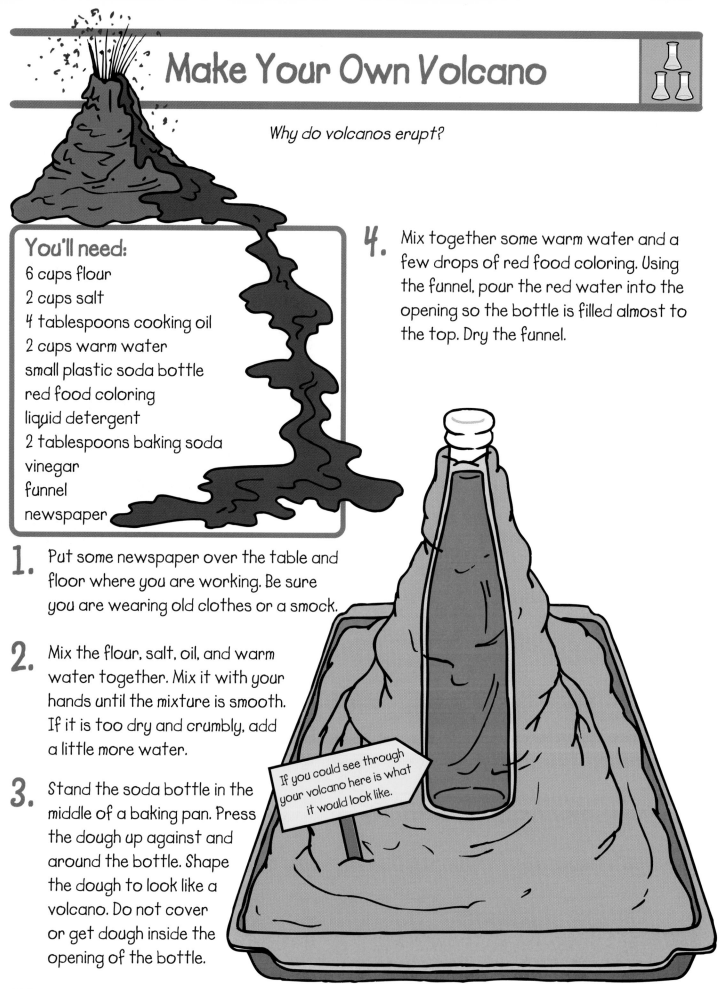

Why do volcanos erupt?

You'll need:
6 cups flour
2 cups salt
4 tablespoons cooking oil
2 cups warm water
small plastic soda bottle
red food coloring
liquid detergent
2 tablespoons baking soda
vinegar
funnel
newspaper

1. Put some newspaper over the table and floor where you are working. Be sure you are wearing old clothes or a smock.

2. Mix the flour, salt, oil, and warm water together. Mix it with your hands until the mixture is smooth. If it is too dry and crumbly, add a little more water.

3. Stand the soda bottle in the middle of a baking pan. Press the dough up against and around the bottle. Shape the dough to look like a volcano. Do not cover or get dough inside the opening of the bottle.

4. Mix together some warm water and a few drops of red food coloring. Using the funnel, pour the red water into the opening so the bottle is filled almost to the top. Dry the funnel.

If you could see through your volcano here is what it would look like.

5. Add six drops of liquid detergent to the bottle. Pour the baking soda through the funnel. Next slowly pour some vinegar into the bottle.

What happens? The volcano "erupts." Red "lava" comes out of the top of the bottle and runs down the sides of the volcano.

Why? When you mix vinegar and baking soda, there is a chemical reaction. It makes carbon dioxide gas. Carbon dioxide makes bubbles, and the bubbles build up in the soda bottle. The bubbles take up space, and when there is no more room inside the bottle, the liquid comes out of the top of the volcano.

Although your volcano was fun to watch, real volcanos are dangerous, powerful, and deadly. In 1815 an eruption in Indonesia killed 92,000 people. And when Krakatoa erupted in 1883, it destroyed 163 Indonesian villages and killed 36,380 people! Dust from the eruption fell more than 3,000 miles away, almost ten days later!

There are 1,343 active volcanos in the world. Right now the largest active volcano is Mauna Loa in Hawaii. It is 75 miles long and 31 miles wide. Between 1843 and 1984, it erupted about once every four years.

Science Sleuth-Volcanos

The center of the earth is very, very hot. It can reach 13,000°! Any rocks at the center of the earth will melt when it is that hot. They become liquid (or *molten*) and are called *magma*.

Magma can even form in the part of the earth's surface that is called the *mantle*. *Magma* is hotter and not as heavy as the rocks that surround it, so it begins to rise to the top of the mantle.

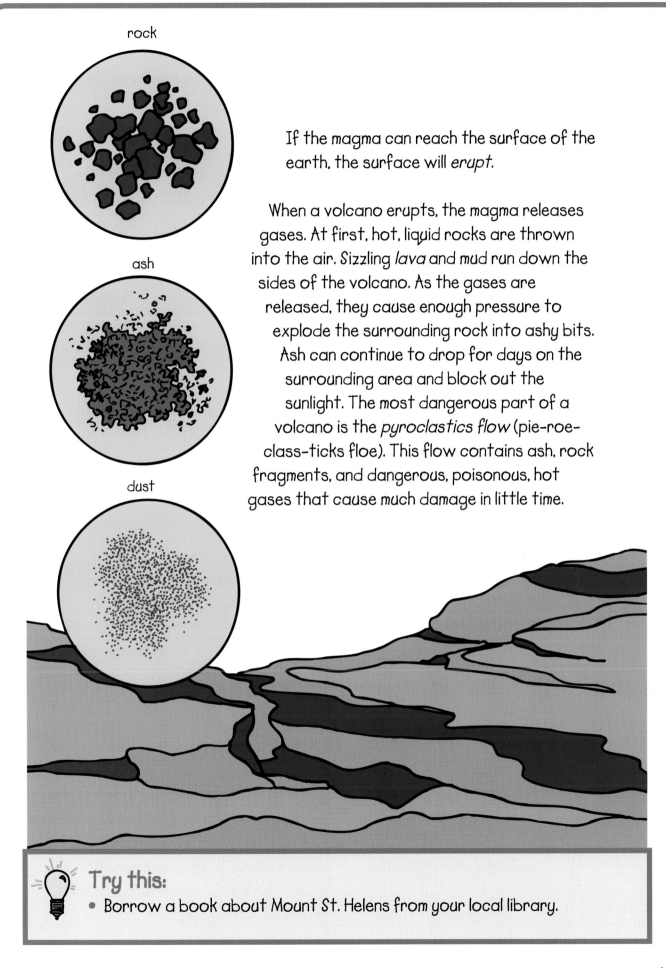

rock

ash

dust

If the *magma* can reach the surface of the earth, the surface will *erupt*.

When a volcano erupts, the *magma* releases gases. At first, hot, liquid rocks are thrown into the air. Sizzling *lava* and mud run down the sides of the volcano. As the gases are released, they cause enough pressure to explode the surrounding rock into ashy bits. Ash can continue to drop for days on the surrounding area and block out the sunlight. The most dangerous part of a volcano is the *pyroclastics flow* (pie-roe-class-ticks floe). This flow contains ash, rock fragments, and dangerous, poisonous, hot gases that cause much damage in little time.

Try this:
- Borrow a book about Mount St. Helens from your local library.

Lemon Soda

How is making soda a scientific process?

You'll need:
baking soda
lemonade

1. Fill a glass halfway with lemonade. Stir $1/2$ teaspoon of baking soda into the lemonade.

2. Drink the lemon soda right away before the bubbles are gone.

What happens? The lemonade gets bubbly, like soda.

Why? Lemons contain citric acid. So does lemonade. Baking soda is made up of sodium, carbon, hydrogen, and oxygen. When these elements combine with the acid, there is a chemical reaction. The chemical reaction gives off the gas carbon dioxide, which makes the bubbles.

Play Dough

Sometimes making toys can be a scientific process.

You'll need:

1 cup flour
$1/3$ cup water
$1/3$ cup salt
1 tablespoon vegetable oil

1. Mix all the ingredients together.

What happens? You make a clay that can be used to sculpt and mold. (Store it in a zippered plastic bag.)

Why? When you make play dough, you act like a scientist. Scientists mix together different substances to make new substances.

Science Sleuth— Chemical Properties

When *you* do an experiment, it is important to observe things. When *you* observe things, you watch what happens. But you also notice what things look like, feel like, smell like, and in some cases, taste like.

Properties help you identify things. A chemical may be a solid, a liquid, or a gas, but its basic properties will always remain the same.

Here's how to tell what something is:

salt   sugar

Taste

Salt and sugar look almost exactly alike when you see them next to each other. And neither one has a smell. You can tell them apart only when you taste them. Taste can be an important chemical property, although *you should NEVER taste something unless you are absolutely sure it is safe!*

apple juice   olive oil

Sometimes things may look the same, but taste and feel different.

apple slice   potato slice

Touch

Sometimes things may look the same, but feel different. If you see a cup of apple juice and a cup of olive oil sitting next to each other, you may think they are the same thing. But if you feel them both, the oil will feel thicker and heavier and will stick to your fingers more.

Smell

If you cut a piece from an apple and a potato, they would look and feel alike. But if you smelled them, you would definitely be able to tell them apart.

 Try this:
- Investigate salt and sugar. Pour a little of each on the table. Can you tell the difference without tasting? Ask a grown-up to try.
- Investigate cooking oil and apple juice. Ask your grown-up helper to pour a little of each into two small cups. Feel them. Can you tell the difference? Are there any other properties that are different?
- Investigate apples and potatoes. How else can you tell them apart besides the way they feel?
- Investigate orange juice, peanut butter, jelly, and yogurt. What kinds of properties make these substances easy to identify?

Making Ginger Ale

What makes ginger ale bubbly?

You'll need:

4 quarts water

3 tablespoons powdered ginger

juice from 1/2 lime

2 1/2 cups sugar

3 tablespoons cream of tartar

1 tablespoon baker's yeast

coffee filter

funnel

clean, empty gallon jug with a cap

3. Mix in the yeast. Put a cover on the pot. Let it sit for six hours.

4. Place the funnel in the top of your gallon jug. Line the funnel with a coffee filter. Do not fill your jug all the way to the top. Leave some space or there won't be enough room for the bubbles! Put the cap on the jug. Put the ginger ale in the refrigerator. Wait two days before you drink it.

1. Pour the water into a pot. (STOP) Ask a grown-up to boil the water on the stove.

2. Add the ginger, lime juice, and sugar. Mix with a spoon until the sugar dissolves. Add the cream of tartar. Mix well again. Let the mixture cool until it is lukewarm.

What happens? You make fizzy ginger ale!

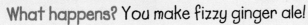

Why? The yeast that you put in your mixture is actually tiny little plants. Yeast plants can't make their own food like other plants. The yeast feeds on the sugar you put in your mixture. Sugar has a lot of energy. Yeast turns sugar into carbon dioxide and alcohol. This is called *fermentation*. When you put the mixture in the refrigerator, the cooler temperature stops the alcohol from being produced in this experiment.

The carbon-dioxide gas makes bubbles. Because the cap is on tight, the bubbles cannot escape into the air, so your ginger ale stays fizzy.

The ginger ale you buy in the store is not made like this. It would take too much yeast. Soda companies pump carbon dioxide into their ginger-ale solutions to make them fizzy.

Caramel

Is caramel the result of a chemical reaction?

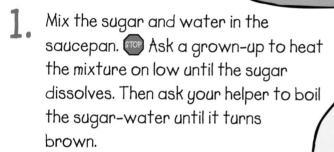

You'll need:
small, heavy-bottomed saucepan
1/4 cup white sugar
2 tablespoons water
2 teaspoons boiling water

1. Mix the sugar and water in the saucepan. **STOP** Ask a grown-up to heat the mixture on low until the sugar dissolves. Then ask your helper to boil the sugar-water until it turns brown.

2. **STOP** Ask your helper to take the pot off the stove and stir the boiling water into the mixture. Let it cool. When the caramel is cool and thick, you can spoon it onto donuts, cookies, apples, or ice cream.

What happens? The sugar solution turns into a caramel sauce when it is heated.

Why? When you boil the sugar, you add heat. The heat energy causes a chemical change in the sugar. That makes the sugar look, feel, and taste different.

Electro-Lemon

Make a battery out of a lemon.

You'll need:

brass thumbtack
steel paper clip
fresh lemon
small flashlight bulb (less than 3 volts)
2 pieces of electrical wire

1. Stick the thumbtack into one side of the lemon. Stick the paper clip into the other side.

2. **STOP** Ask a grown-up to attach both pieces of electrical wire to the bulb. Connect one wire to the thumbtack. Connect the other wire to the paper clip.

What happens? The bulb lights up.

Why? Electricity is made when some chemicals react with each other. Batteries contain these chemicals. One chemical in a battery is called the *electrolyte.* It is connected to two *electrodes,* which are usually some kind of metal substances. In the lemon battery, the acid in the lemon is the electrolyte. The thumbtack and the paper clip are the electrodes. The electrolyte has a chemical reaction with the electrodes. This creates electrical energy. The energy travels through the wires attached to the bulb and makes it light up.

Blue Clouds

How does baking cause a chemical reaction?

You'll need:
4 egg whites
2 cups sugar
blue food coloring (or another color you like)
cream of tartar

1. **STOP** Ask a grown-up to preheat the oven to 200°.

2. **STOP** With help, beat the egg whites with an electric mixer until they become frothy. Beat in the cream of tartar at medium speed. Gradually add 2 tablespoons of sugar.

3. When soft peaks form, add 1 tablespoon of sugar and beat on high speed. When stiff peaks form, slowly raise the mixer, and gradually beat in the rest of the sugar. Add a few drops of food coloring. Beat the mixture until it is very stiff and glossy.

SUGAR

4. Pour the mixture into the plastic bag. 🛑 Cut off one of the bottom corners of the bag. Squeeze the bag to make small mounds on a cookie sheet.

5. 🛑 Bake the clouds for one hour.

What happens? The egg whites become big and fluffy and solid after you whisk and bake them.

Why? When you whisk the eggs, air molecules get caught inside the mixture. The more air molecules that get trapped inside, the more foamy the eggs become. When you put the clouds in the oven, the heat makes the air bubbles get even bigger. The heat also causes a chemical change that makes the egg whites become solid.

Rising Dough

What makes bread soft and fluffy?

You'll need:

2 cups whole-wheat flour
1 cup all-purpose flour
1 package dry yeast
1 cup milk
1 tablespoon honey
1 tablespoon butter or margarine
1 teaspoon salt

1. Mix the yeast with $1/2$ cup whole-wheat flour and $1/2$ cup all-purpose flour.

2. **STOP** Ask a grown-up to heat the milk, honey, margarine, and salt in a saucepan to warm. Heat it slowly so the margarine melts.

3. When the margarine has melted, add the liquid mixture to the flour mixture. Mix until it is well-blended.

4. Stir in the rest of the flour, bit by bit, until the dough is stiff. (You may not need to use all the flour.)

5. Sprinkle some flour on the tabletop. Knead the dough on the tabletop for ten minutes–ask your grown-up helper to show you how.

6. Place the dough into a large bowl. Cover it with a towel or cloth. Put the bowl in a warm area for about an hour and a half. When you uncover it, the dough will be doubled in size!

7. Put the dough on the floured table again. Punch it down (that means to lightly punch the dough until it shrinks in size).

8. Grease a loaf pan. Put the dough in the loaf pan. Set the loaf pan in a warm place. Cover it with a cloth again. Leave the dough this way for about an hour.

9. 🛑 Bake the bread at 375° for 45 to 50 minutes.

What happens? When you leave the dough covered in a warm place, it grows larger.

Why? The yeast used in this experiment makes carbon dioxide when it is added to the mixture and then baked. The carbon dioxide is released as gas bubbles. The gas bubbles push the surrounding dough up and out, making the dough rise.

Finding a Lab

If you can't decide where to set up your laboratory, find a room where you can easily get to these things:

- a sink
- a table
- windows you can open
- a sunny area
- a stove nearby, if your experiment uses one
- a refrigerator nearby, if you need ice for your experiment

Filling Your Lab

You can start collecting all kinds of materials and supplies for your lab. Here are some ideas for your laboratory kit:

jars with lids, in different sizes	balloons
rubber bands	string
plastic bowls	cardboard
plastic wrap	chopsticks
spoons	scissors
measuring cups	paper
tape	plastic drinking straws
a ruler	soil
a watch	plastic cups
plastic bottles, in different sizes	paper towels

Planning Your Magic Show

Once you've learned the Science Magic experiments, then what?
There's more to fooling the eye than just knowing the tricks.

- Practice, practice, practice. You should be able to do your trick quickly so no one can figure out how it works.

- Collect your equipment. Each magic trick needs certain props. Be sure you have everything you need in one place.

- Put together a costume. Make a magic wand. Make your "stage." (Use as much black as possible. Cover the wall behind you with a black sheet; put a black tablecloth over your table. Black makes it harder for your audience to see how you do your tricks.)

- While you perform your magic, keep talking to your audience. Try to distract them, so they don't notice secrets you don't want them to see.

- When you are performing a trick, you may want to have your assistant wave a scarf or tell a joke, so the audience will watch him and not you.

- Change the names of the tricks. The names in this book will help you remember how the tricks work. But if you tell your audience those names, they will figure out your magic. For instance, change "Trap Door" to "Disappearing Box."

- Never tell anyone the secrets of your magic tricks!!

Answer Key

Answers to the true/false questions on page 28:

A. False—the small intestines are 20 feet long and the large intestines are 5 feet long.
B. True
C. True
D. False—it takes 14 muscles to make you smile.
E. True—it was called phrenology.

F. False—oxygen makes blood red. The blood in your veins lacks oxygen.
G. True—but only 100,000 of these hairs are on your head.
H. False—each eyelash lasts about 150 days.
I. True
J. True
K. True

Answers to the fill-in-the-blank questions on page 28:

1. 100
2. 20,000
3. 100,000
4. 100,000
5. 2/3
6. 26 billion, 50 trillion

7. 2, 20
8. 60,000
9. 3 days
10. 977
11. 69
12. 30 billion

Answer Key

Answers to the true/false questions on page 84:

A. True

B. True

C. True

D. False—they touch hands.

E. False—it sticks out its tongue.

F. False—only female mosquitoes bite.

G. True

H. True

I. True

J. False—Charles V had seven pet seals.

K. True

L. False—they had a pet orangutan.

Answers to the fill-in-the-blank questions on page 84:

1. blue whale
2. giraffe
3. anaconda
4. ostrich
5. cockroach
6. hummingbird
7. elephants
8. 2,000
9. noses
10. parrot
11. alligator
12. turkey
13. Emily Spinach
14. bobcat, donkey, raccoons
15. 200 million

Answers to the matching problems on page 89:

Animal baby names:

a. 5 (or 2)
b. 8
c. 6
d. 9
e. 12 (or 1 or 15)
f. 10
g. 2 (or 5)
h. 11
i. 7
j. 1 (or 12 or 15)
k. 4
l. 13
m. 3
n. 15 (or 1 or 12)
o. 16
p. 14

Animal group names:

a. 5
b. 6
c. 7
d. 8
e. 3
f. 1
g. 4
h. 12
i. 10
j. 2
k. 13
l. 9
m. 20
n. 16
o. 11
p. 19
q. 21
r. 15
s. 22
t. 14
u. 18
v. 17

Glossary

Air pressure The force of air pressing down on something.

Atom The tiny particle that makes up everything; it is the smallest part of an element that still behaves like that element.

Biology The study of living things.

Cell membrane The thin "skin" on the outside of the cell. It controls what moves in and out of the cell.

Center of gravity The place where the weight of an object seems to be concentrated.

Chemistry The study of how chemicals react with each other.

Chlorophyll A green chemical in plants that aids in photosynthesis.

Chromosomes The parts of a cell that carry genes.

Compound A substance made by at least two elements that are chemically bonded together.

Glossary

Condensation When a gas changes to a liquid.

Conduct When electricity or heat travels through an object.

Conductor Anything that will let electricity or heat pass through.

Cones Parts of the eye that tell one color from another.

Current When electrons flow around a circuit (this has a negative charge).

Cytoplasm The jellylike substance inside a cell that holds chemicals and nutrients. This is where a cell does its work.

Electricity A kind of energy. It is made when electrons move between atoms.

Electron A particle that is part of an atom. Electrons are negatively charged.

Element A substance that cannot be broken down into smaller substances.

Evaporation When liquid changes to a gas.

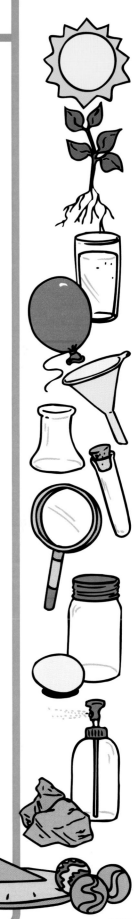

Glossary

Force A push or pull on an object.

Friction When two objects rub against each other. Sometimes friction will cause heat. It also causes objects that are moving to slow down.

Gas A substance, often invisible, that spreads out to fill its container. The molecules spread out more in gases than in other substances.

Gene Part of a cell that decides what physical traits a person will have.

Genetics The study of why living things look and act a certain way.

Gravity A force that pulls things toward each other. Your feet stay on the ground because of the force (gravity) between your body and the earth.

Inertia When an object does not change its movement. If it is moving, it is hard to stop it from moving. If it is still, it is hard to make it move. Heavy things have more inertia than light things.

Glossary

Lever A bar that rests on a support; when you push down on one end, the other end is lifted. It is called a simple machine.

Lift An upward force. When air moves over the wings of a plane or bird very fast, it keeps the plane or bird in the air. This is lift. The air pressure above the wing is less than the air pressure below the wing.

Lightning The spark that is made when electrons move through the air.

Liquid A substance that is wet. It can be poured, and it takes the shape of the container it is poured into.

Magma The liquid rock that is beneath the earth's surface.

Matter Anything that takes up space and has mass or weight.

Molecules At least two atoms that are chemically bonded together; the smallest part of a compound.

Glossary

Nocturnal animals Animals that sleep during the day and are awake at night.

Nucleus The part of a cell that controls everything the cell does. The DNA is found here.

Osmosis The movement of liquid through a cell membrane.

Photosynthesis When a plant makes food (sugar), oxygen, and energy out of carbon dioxide and water. It needs light to do this.

Pneumatic machines Machines that use compressed air to make their parts move.

Protons Particles found in the nucleus of an atom. They have a positive charge.

Solid A substance that keeps its shape.

Vibrate To move back and forth regularly.

Xylem The tubes in a plant that deliver water from the roots to the leaves.

Yeast A fungus that is used to make bread.

INDEX

INDEX

INDEX

INDEX